Anonymous

Great Southern Railway

A trunk line, between the North and the tropics, to within ninety miles of Havana,

connecting at the nearest possible point with the West Indies, Central America and

South America

Anonymous

Great Southern Railway
A trunk line, between the North and the tropics, to within ninety miles of Havana, connecting at the nearest possible point with the West Indies, Central America and South America

ISBN/EAN: 9783337315795

Printed in Europe, USA, Canada, Australia, Japan

Cover: Foto ©Andreas Hilbeck / pixelio.de

More available books at **www.hansebooks.com**

GREAT

SOUTHERN RAILWAY,

A TRUNK LINE,

BETWEEN THE NORTH AND THE TROPICS,

TO WITHIN

NINETY MILES OF HAVANA,

CONNECTING AT THE

Nearest Possible Point

WITH THE WEST INDIES, CENTRAL AMERICA,

AND SOUTH AMERICA.

ERRATA.

Page 18, line 12, for " as " read " are."
" 20, last line, for " 11 " read " 10.'
" 23, line 27, for " exceding " read " exceeding."
" 33 line 7, for " Fronaudina " read " Fernandina."
" 34, line 2, for " siral " read " sisal."
" 35, line 31, for " demonstrate " read " demonstrates."
" 36, line 3, for " insure " read " insures."
" 36, line 11, after " which " read " mark."
" 42, line 25, for those " read " thence."
" 43, line 14, " all " should commence a new sentence.
" 44, line 14, strike out " the."
" 45, line 22, for " our ' road " one.'
" 46, line 9, insert " for " before " practically."
" 46, line 10, strike out " for."
" 46, line 15, for " 5,000 000 " read " 4,000,000."
" 49, line 5, for " Osgechee " read " Ogeechee."
" 49, line 20, for " and " read " Jacksonville."
" 52, line 24, for " quality " read " quality."
" 54, line 29, for " for " read " of."
" 56, line 18, strike out " of."
" 56, line 22, before " that " insert " is."
" 61, line 29, for " it " read " its."
" 65, line 23, for " Frsck." read " Fredk."
" 69, line 16, for " tranported " read " transported."
" 72, line 22, for " Rautan " read " Ruatan."
" 73, line 4, for " applies " read " apples."
" 73, line 30, for " in " read " on."
" 75, line 14, for " $509,138 60 " read " $509,109.60."
" 78, line 15, for " Terra " read " Terre."
" 79, line 10, for " Mora " read " Moro."
" 80, line 11, for " $226,119,528 " read " $225,980,689."
" 111, line 23, for " mango-guava " read " mango, guava."
" 112, line 30, for " Blanguilla " read " Blanquilla."
" 114, line 17, for " main " read " mail."
" 117, line 2, for " manyfold " read " many fold."
" 119, line 5, after " commerce " insert will."
" 120, line 16, for " $72,617,611 " read " $72.637,611."
" 120, line 16, for " $1 040 518 " read " $1,040.647."
" 120, line 18, for " $121,645,011 " read " $124,665,041."
" 121, line 18, for " port " read " fact."
" 126 line 17, for " withing " read " within."
" 126, line 19, for " for " read " far "
" 132, line 16, read instead, " $107,395,192," " 388,658,507," " 497,143,729."
" 132, line 22, strike out " and."
" 133, line 30, for " Venzuela " read " Venezuela."
" 135, line 18, read instead, " 577 329,126," " 702,519,526."
" 137, line 14, strike out " the."
" 138, line 26, for " 775 " read " 675."
" 138, line 29, for " 411 " read " 446."
" 139, line 1, after " New " read " York."
" 144, line 28, for " close " read " closer."
" 148, line 12, after " shall " insert " have "
" 154, line 27, for " $3,600,000 " read " $3,600,000,000."
" 163, line 29, after " for " insert " the "
" 171, line 7, for " Grand Total " read " Total Exports."
" 186, line 11, for " even " read " ever."
" 191, line 1, for " 35 " read " 135."

INCORPORATION OF THE GREAT SOUTHERN RAILWAY COMPANY.

The Great Southern Railway Company of Georgia.—The Great Southern Railway Company was incorporated by an Act of the Legislature of the State of Georgia, approved October 17th, 1870, with general and special powers to construct and operate a railroad from Millen to the St. Mary's River, there to connect with the road constructed in Florida. In connection with existing roads, the line thus forms a direct through line between all the Southern, Western and Northern States and the West Indies, Central America, and South America.

The Great Southern Railway Company of Florida.—The Great Southern Railway Company was incorporated by an Act of the Legislature of the State of Florida, approved February 19th, 1870, with all the general powers usually conferred upon railroad corporations, and with special powers to construct and operate a railroad from the St. Mary's River, on the northern boundary of Florida, to the most southerly available harbor of the State, and to own and operate, in connection with the road, and as an integral part of the Company's line, steamships and other sea-going vessels to Cuba and the other West India Islands and South America.

Length of Road.—The length of the road in Georgia is 170 miles; the length of the road in Florida is 550 miles, making a total length of road of 720 miles of main line, with a branch of 126 miles to Tampa on the west side of the peninsula of Florida.

OBJECTS AND ADVANTAGES OF THE ROAD.—The Great Southern Railway is designed to connect the entire railway system of the United States with Cuba, the other West Indies, Southern Mexico, Central America and South America by the most direct and close railway and steamship connections that can possibly be opened.

The line begins at Millen, on the Georgia Central road, where an air line railroad running due south from New York city strikes the Georgia Central, and runs thence due south to Key West, the southernmost point in the United States.

Key West is within ninety miles of Havana. Thus the water communication with Cuba is reduced to a ferry across the Strait of Florida ; and that to Hayti, San Domingo, and Jamaica and the other West India Islands, Southern Mexico, Central America and South America is 1,155 miles less than the now usual routes from New York.

FLORIDA CHARTER.

AN ACT

TO INCORPORATE THE GREAT SOUTHERN RAILWAY COMPANY, AND
TO PERFECT ONE OF THE PUBLIC WORKS OF THE STATE.

WHEREAS, It is the true intent and meaning of an act of
the Legislature of Florida, entitled an Act to Provide for and
Encourage a Liberal System of Internal Improvements in
this State, approved January 6, 1855, and of an act entitled
An Act to Perfect the Public Works of the State, approved
June 24, 1869, and all amendments to the said acts, that new
routes of rail and water communication in addition to those
designated in said acts, shall be opened and established;
AND WHEREAS, The public policy of this State favors the
most liberal legislation in aid of such individuals or corporations as shall have for their object the development of the
resources of the State, the establishment of external and
internal commerce, the promotion of domestic trade and
industry, and the general improvement of the country;
therefore,

The people of the State of Florida, represented in Senate
and Assembly, do enact as follows: SECTION 1. That Harrison
Reed, George B. Carse, William H. Gleason, Thomas W.
Osborn, Marcellus L. Stearns, Horatio Jenkins, Jr., Charles
M. Hamilton, Edward H. Reed, William J. Purman, Charles
H. Pearce, and Josiah T. Walls, of the State of Florida, and
A. C. Osborn of the State of New York, and such other
persons as may become associated with them by becoming
stockholders in said company, their successors and assigns,
are hereby created and shall forever be a body politic and
corporate, by the name and style of the Great Southern

Railway Company, and by such name shall be capable in law to purchase, receive, hold, and convey and quietly enjoy lands and tenements, goods and chattels, property of every kind and effects, whatsoever the same may be, and the same to grant, sell, and mortgage, and convey and dispose of, to sue and be sued, to plead and be impleaded, to contract and be contracted with, to make a common seal, and at pleasure to alter or break the same, to ordain, establish, and put in execution such by-laws and regulations as may be deemed necessary and expedient for the government of and for conducting the business of said corporation, not being in conflict with the laws of the United States and of the State of Florida.

Sec. 2. That this company shall have the right to construct equip, and operate a line of railroad which shall commence at some point at or near King's Ferry on the St. Mary's River, in the State of Florida, which point shall be determined and located by the board of directors of said company, thence to the city of Jacksonville or by way of Jacksonville, thence in a southerly direction, via Palatka, by the most practical route, to the most southern available harbor on the coast or keys of Florida, to be determined by the board of directors ; and said company may build and operate such branch road or roads as may be necessary to establish connection with the more remote parts of the State of Florida, and to perfect an important part of the system of internal improvements in this State.

Sec. 3. That the said company may own and sail steamships and other sea going vessels in connection with said railroad to any port or ports of the West India Islands and South America, or of the United States, and such line of steamships or other vessels shall be considered to be an integral part of said railroad, and in connection with said road shall constitute one continuous through line for the transportation of freight and passengers between the St. Mary's river and the West India Islands and South America, to be known as the Great Southern Railway Company, and said company shall have the right to construct and operate lines of telegraph on the route of said railroad and its branches, connecting with any shore or cable lines of telegraph said company may establish.

Sec. 4. That the capital stock of said company be ten millions (10,000,000) of dollars, divided into shares of one hundred dollars each. Books of subscription shall be opened within sixty days after the passage of this act, under the charge and supervision of Henry D. Cook, of the City of Washington, and George N. Hubbard and Samuel L. Merrill, of the State of New York, who are hereby appointed commissioners for that purpose, and the said commissioners, or a majority of them who shall act, are hereby authorized and empowered to receive subscriptions to the stock to said company, but said commissioners shall not on their own account subscribe to the capital stock: *Provided*, That said books of subscription may be opened and subscriptions made either in the State of Florida, or in the city of New York, or both. The books of subscription shall be kept open until the whole capital stock is subscribed.

Sec. 5. That when all the capital stock is subscribed, notice shall be given in some newspaper published in Florida and in the city of New York, that a meeting of the stockholders will be held at the time and place designated in said notice, for the purpose of electing directors, who shall be chosen from the stockholders of said company. Stockholders shall be entitled to one vote for each share of the stock held by them, and stockholders may vote by proxy. A majority of votes shall be necessary to constitute a choice of directors.

The directors so elected shall continue in office one year, or until new directors are duly elected. The directors so elected shall from their own body choose a president, and in like manner in each and every year the directors and president shall be chosen. Vacancies which may occur in their body between the periods of the annual elections may be filled by said directors; *Provided*, That if, from any cause, there should be no election, the corporation shall not be dissolved, but the directors and other officers then in office shall continue in office with all the powers herein mentioned until the election of new directors shall take place.

SEC. 6. That said directors or a majority of them may make such rules and regulations and such by-laws for the payment of stock, and for all other purposes, as they may deem expedient and proper. Said company, may, by their directors, elect and employ all other officers, such as secretary, treasurer, agents, engineers, and superintendent, and discharge them at pleasure.

SEC. 7. That in the construction and operation of said road the said company shall have the right to build all bridges necessary to enable the railroad or any of its branches to cross any rivers or streams; but in crossing navigable rivers or streams, suitable draws shall be constructed to admit and provide for the passage of all steamboats and other water-craft usually navigating such rivers or streams, and said draws shall at all times be kept in good order, and shall be opened whenever necessary to the commerce of said rivers or streams.

SEC. 8. The said company shall have the right and privilege to construct said railroad with a branch road or roads for the transportation of passengers, goods, wares, and merchandise, and all other articles whatsoever, through any of the lands of the State of Florida; and the right of way is hereby given for the same two hundred feet in width, with the right to take stone, timber, earth, and material, from any lands belonging to the State, in the construction, operation and repair of said railroad and its branches.

SEC. 9. That the president and directors of said company are hereby authorized to contract for and receive conveyances of land, timber, and other materials which may be required by the directors in the construction, operation, and repair of said road, and when the owner and the company cann ot agree upon the price, or when the owner is an infant, non-resident, or *non compos mentis*, then it shall be lawful for the president of said company to apply to the sheriff of the county in which said lands are located, who shall summon a jury of three disinterested free-holders, a majority of whom shall be authorized to assess the damages and return their award or judgment to the term of the circuit court of the county in which the said lands or other property may be located, which shall be entered by the clerk as the judgment of the court, and execution may issue thereon for the amount of said judgment and costs. Before proceeding to the discharge of the duties herein required, the jurors summoned shall take an oath of affirmation, to be administered by the sherriff, that they will well and truly inquire into and to the best of their judgment assess the damages to the owner or owners of said land or materials by means of the construction.

SEC. 10. The property so assessed and paid for by said railroad company in conformity with the provisions of this act, and all donations from any source for the same, shall forever afterward belong to and become the property of said railroad company, its successors and assigns, in fee simple in proportion to the number of shares held by the stock-holders respectively. Subscription to the capital stock of said railroad company may be made in land, labor, and material, upon such terms as may be agreed upon by the directors and the owner or owners thereof.

SEC. 11. That the directors of said company shall have the right to demand and receive such prices and sums for fare and the transportation of freight, produce, and merchandise as may be authorized and fixed by the by-laws of said company.

SEC. 12. That in order to promote the speedy success of the public work contemplated by this act, there is hereby granted to the said company, with consent of the Trustees of the Internal Improvement Fund, the same number of acres of land per mile of the lands known as swamp and overflowed lands, granted to the State by act of Congress of September 28, 1850, as may hereafter be granted to said com-pany by the United States, in aid of the construction of the proposed line of railroad and branches, and the said lands are hereby granted, subject to the provisions of the act of Congress of September 28, 1850, granting the same to the State ; and said lands shall be selected by the said company from those located nearest to the line of said railroad.

SEC. 13. That said company may issue coupon bonds of such denomination and value, and bearing such rates of interest, and payable at such time and places as the board of directors may determine, and may issue such other evidences of indebtedness as the said board of directors may determine, and said bonds and other evidences of indebtedness shall be as a lien or mortgage, first on the road beds, iron, equipment, work-shops. depots. and franchises, both corporate and of

13

use, of the said company, and second on the lands of the said company.

SEC. 14. That Sections 20, 21, 30, 33, 34, 35, 36, 38 and 39,* of An Act entitled an act to provide for the Creation of Corporations and to Prescribe their general Powers and Liabilities, approved August 8, 1868, are hereby made specially applicable to the said company, for all the purposes of its corporation, and shall be deemed and held a part of this act, and all acts and parts of acts heretofore passed, in any way interfering or inconsistent with this act, in case any rights and powers created thereunder have not vested by law, are hereby repealed.

SEC. 15. That the company shall have succession for ninety-nine years; that no stockholder's property shall be liable for any greater sum than the unpaid amount of stock for which he has subscribed; that this act shall be deemed and held a public act, and the courts of this State shall take judicial notice thereof without special pleading.

Approved February 19, 1870.

---

* SEC. 20. The stock of every corporation shall be deemed personal estate, and shall be transferable in the manner prescribed in the by-laws or regulations of the company, but no shares shall be transferred until all previous assessments thereon shall have been fully paid in.

SEC. 21. All bodies, corporate, as contemplated by this statute, by any suit at law, in any court having competent jurisdiction, may sue for, recover, and receive from their respective members, all arrears or other debts, dues, or other demands which now, or hereafter, may be owing to them, in like manner, mode and form as they might sue for and recover the same from any other person.

SEC. 30. It shall be lawful for any corporation to convey lands by deed sealed with the common seal of said corporation, and signed by the president or presiding member, or trustee of said corporation, and such deed when so executed shall be recorded by the recorder in the county clerk's office of the county where the land lies in like manner with other deeds, and no further proof shall be deemed necessary to commit the same to record.

SEC. 33. The treasurer or cashier of every corporation shall keep an accurate list of its stockholders, with the number of shares owned by each, which shall at all times upon written application by any stockholder be open to his inspection, and if such officer refuse to exhibit such list, he shall forfeit fifty dollars for each offense, to be deducted from his pay or salary.

SEC. 34. When a majority in number or interest of the members of a corporation desire to close their concerns, they may apply by petition to the circuit court, setting forth the grounds of their appplication, and the court on due notice by publication for a reasonable period by them given to all parties interested, may hear the matter, and for reasonable and just cause decree a dissolution of the corporation, and the corporation so dissolved shall be deemed and held extinct in all respects as if their charter had expired by its own limitation, and the settlement of the affairs of such corporation so dissolved shall be managed as prescribed in cases of voluntary dissolution.

SEC. 35. All corporations shall continue bodies corporate for the term of three years after the time of dissolution from any cause, for the purpose of prosecuting or defending suits by or against them, and enabling them to gradually settle their concerns, to dispose of and convey their property and to divide their capital stock, but for no other purpose.

SEC. 36. No body of persons acting as a corporation under this act, shall be permitted to set up the want of a legal organization as a defense to an action against them as a corporation, nor shall any person sued on a contract made with such corporation, or sued for an injury to its property, or a wrong done to its interests, be permitted to set up a want of such legal organization in his defense.

SEC. 38. Any corporation organized and put into successful operation under this act, shall have exclusive privileges for the purposes of its creation for the term of twenty years from the date the corporation commences to carry out in good faith the terms of its articles of incorporation ; *Provided, however,* That this investment shall not so operate as to divest any future Legislature of those powers of government which are inherent and essential attributes of sovereignty, to wit, the power to create revenue for public purposes, to provide for the common defense, to provide safe and convenient ways for the public necessity and convenience, and to take private property for public use, and the like.

SEC. 39. The records of any company incorporated under the provisions of this statute, or copies thereof duly authenticated by the signature of the president and secretary of such company under the corporate seal shall be competent evidence in any court.

GEORGIA CHARTER.

AN ACT

TO INCORPORATE THE GREAT SOUTHERN RAILWAY COMPANY.

WHEREAS, A company has been incorporated by an Act of the State of Florida for the purpose of constructing and operating a railroad through the entire extent of the peninsula of Florida, from the St. Mary's River on the north, to Key Bischyne Bay on the south; and also for the purpose of operating a line of steamers across the strait of Florida, between the southernmost accessible point of the peninsula of Florida to Cuba and the other West India Islands. *And, whereas,* The opening of a direct connection between such through line to Cuba and the railroads of Georgia, will be of incalculable benefit to this State, by opening across a large and valuable portion of its territory that has hitherto been unprovided with railroad advantages, a grand trunk line between the West India Islands and the entire North and Northwest; therefore,

SECTION 1. *Be it enacted by the Senate and House of Representatives of the State of . Georgia, in General Assembly met, and it is hereby enacted by the authority of the same,* That A. C. Osborn and A. C. Burke of the State of New York; M. L. Stearns and Horatio Jenkins, Jr., of the State of Florida; M. H. Alberger of the City of Washington, D.C., and W. P. Rhodes, W. H. Stallings, W. C. Crittenden, L. A. Bond and Samuel Levy of the State of Georgia, and such other persons as may become associated with them by becoming stockholders in said company, their successors and assigns, are hereby created, and shall forever be a body corporate and politic by the name and style of the Great Southern Railway Company, and by such name shall be capable in law to purchase, receive, hold and convey, and quietly enjoy lands and tenements, goods and chattels, property of every kind and effects whatsoever, necessary to the building, equipping and running said road, and the same to grant, sell and mortgage, and convey, and dispose of, to sue and be sued, to plead and be impleaded, to contract and be contracted with, to make a common seal, and at pleasure to alter or break the same, to ordain, establish and put in circulation such by-laws and regulations as may be deemed necessary and expedient for the government of, and for conducting the business of said corporation, not being in conflict with the laws of the United States and the State of Georgia.

Sec. 2. That said company shall have the right, and is hereby authorized and empowered to construct, equip and operate a railroad and telegraph line from Millen, in Burke county, in as nearly a straight line as the topography of the country will allow—said line to be determined by a competent Engineer to be appointed by said company—to the St. Mary's River, there to connect with the road of the Great Southern Railway Company of Florida; and said company is hereby authorized and empowered to cross railroads and other roads, and to connect with railroads which it may cross, by switch or otherwise, as the interests of the trade may demand.

Sec. 3. That the capital stock of said company shall be three millions of dollars, ($3,000,000) divided into shares of one hundred dollars each ; but said company may, by a vote of two-thirds of its board of directors, increase its capital to four millions ($4,000,000) of dollars. Every person holding the stock of said company shall be liable for all assessments

2

or installments that may fall due; and if any assessment or instalment is not paid when due, the stock upon such assessment or installment shall be liable to forfeiture to the company, and shall be so forfeited if so declared by a vote of the board of directors, sixty days previous notice having been given, in writing, to the holder of such stock. Books of subscription shall be opened within sixty days after the passage of this Act, under the charge and supervision of J. W. Clift, of the State of Georgia, T. W. Osborn, of the State of Florida, and Julius E. Ludden, of the State of New York, who are hereby appointed commissioners for that purpose; and the said commissioners, or a majority of them, who shall act as hereby authorized and empowered to open books and receive subscriptions to the capital stock of said company : *Provided*, That said books of subscription may be opened and subscriptions made either in the State of Georgia, or the city of New York, or in both. Subscriptions may be made to the capital stock of said company in lands, labor or materials, upon such terms as may be agreed upon by the board of directors and the owners.

Sec. 4. That when two-thirds of the capital stock is subscribed, notice shall be given in some newspaper published in Georgia, and in the city of New York, that a meeting of the stockholders will be held at the time and place designated in said notice, which place may be either in Georgia or New York, for the purpose of electing directors, who shall be chosen from the stockholders of said company. Stockholders shall be entitled to one vote for each share of the stock held by them, and stockholders may vote by proxy. A majority of votes cast shall be necessary to constitute a choice of directors. The directors so elected shall continue in office one year or until new directors are duly elected. The directors so elected shall, from their own body, choose a President, and in like manner in each and every year the directors and President shall be chosen. Vacancies which may occur in their bodies between the periods of the annual elections may be filled by the directors : *Provided*, That if from any cause there shall be no election, the corporation shall not be dissolved, but the directors and other officers then in office shall continue in office with all the powers herein mentioned, until the election of new directors shall take place.

SEC. 5. That said directors, or a majority of them, may make such rules and regulations and such by-laws for the payment of stock and for all other purposes as they may deem expedient and proper. Said company, by their electors, may elect and employ all other officers, such as secretary, treasurer, agents, engineer and superintendents, and dis-charge them at pleasure.

SEC. 6. That in the construction and operation of said road the said company shall have the right to build all bridges necessary to enable the railroad to cross any rivers or streams ; but in crossing navigable rivers or streams suitable draws shall be constructed to admit and provide for the passage of all steamboats and other water-crafts usually navigating such rivers or streams, and said draws shall at all times be kept in good order, and shall be open whenever necessary for the commerce of such rivers and streams.

SEC. 7. That said company shall have power to cross railroads, and other roads, and to select and take, buy, hold, or receive as a donation, such piece or pieces of land as it may deem necessary for the construction of said road, or the location of its depots or works. And in all cases where the question of the right-of-way arises, or when the said company shall take possesion of any land, timber, earth, stones, or

other material for the construction or keeping in repair of
the same, or any part thereof, and the parties cannot agree
as to the value of the damages, the owners thereof shall select a man, and the company shall select a man, who shall be
disinterested persons, and, if the two cannot agree, they
shall select a third, and the three shall assess the damages
to be paid by the said company. The men thus selected to
assess the damages shall be sworn to take into consideration
an account of the prospective value of the road to the land
through or near which it may run. And upon payment by
said company of the damages assessed as aforesaid, the fee
simple title to such lands, timber, earth, stones, or other material taken, shall vest in the said company: *Provided*, That,
the right-of-way shall in no case embrace more than one
hundred feet in width on each side of the track of said railroad, and that the construction of said road shall in no case
be hindered, impeded or delayed by reason of any question
of damages or unsettled claims.

Sec. 8. That the directors of said company shall have the
right to demand and receive such prices and sums for fare
and transportation of freight, produce and merchandise as
may be authorized and fixed by said company, not to exceed
five cents per mile for travel, and one cent per mile for
freight.

Sec. 9. That said company are hereby authorized, if it be
found necessary for the construction, equipment, or keeping
in repair of said road, to issue bonds of such denomination
and value, and bearing such rates of interest, and payable at
such times and places as the Board of Directors may
determine, and such other evidences of indebtedness as the
said board may determine.

Sec. 11. That said company shall begin the construction

of said road within two years after the passage of this Act, and complete the same within ten years.

Sec. 11. That said company is hereby authorized and empowered to unite and consolidate its stock, and road, and franchises, and connect with the Great Southern Railway Company, incorporated under the laws of the State of Florida, to such an extent, and on such terms, as it may deem expedient; and, in case of such consolidation, such consolidated company shall be invested with all the rights and privileges conferred by this Act, and shall be subject to all limitations and restrictions herein imposed.

Sec. 12. That no stockholder's property shall be liable for any greater sum than the unpaid amount of stock for which he has subscribed; that this Act shall be deemed and held a public Act, and the courts of the State shall take judicial notice thereof without special pleading.

Sec. 13. That when as much as ten miles of said road is finished and in complete running order, and the Governor is satisfied of that fact, it shall be his duty to place the endorsement of the State on the bonds of said company, for the amount of twelve thousand dollars for every mile then completed, and a like amount for every mile afterwards completed; and the faith of the State shall be bound for the payment of the bonds so endorsed, and shall constitute a lien on said railroad and all its property, real and personal of superior dignity to any other lien or encumbrance, without regard to date; and all the property of the company shall be vested in the State by such endorsement, so far as to authorize the Government to seize and sell the same for the payment of the bonds thus endorsed by the State, or the interest accruing thereon, whenever the road shall fail to pay the same; and the Governor may, in his discretion, run said road and pay the net profits towards the liquidation of any such debt; and if it should become necessary for the Governor to sell any of the property of said company for the purposes aforesaid, he shall sell the same in such manner, and on such terms, as he may deem best for all concerned. Said company shall not sell or in any manner dispose of the bonds so endorsed for less than ninety cents on the dollar.

SEC. 14. That all laws and parts of laws, heretofore enacted, that effect or are inconsistent with the provisions of this Act, are hereby declared inoperative and void, so far as they effect or are inconsistent with the provisions of this Act.

Approved October 17, 1870.

A BILL

TO AUTHORIZE THE GREAT SOUTHERN RAILWAY COMPANY TO CONSOLIDATE WITH THE GREAT SOUTHERN RAILWAY COMPANY OF GEORGIA.

SECTION 1. *The People of the State of Florida represented in Senate and Assembly, do enact as follows :* That the Great Southern Railway Company is hereby authorized to unite and consolidate its stock, road and franchises, and connect with the Great Southern Railway, incorporated under the laws of the State of Georgia, to such an extent and on such terms as it may deem expedient ; and in case of such consolidation, such consolidated company shall be invested with all the rights and privileges conferred by this Act, and the Courts of the State shall take judicial notice thereof.

Approved January 24, 1874.

RIGHT OF WAY.

The following act of Congress gives the company the right

of way through the public lands of Florida. The act has been complied with. As there are no United States lands in Georgia the act does not apply to that State.

AN ACT

GRANTING THE RIGHT OF WAY THROUGH THE PUBLIC LAND FOR THE CONSTRUCTION OF A RAILROAD AND TELEGRAPH IN FLORIDA.

Be it enacted by the Senate and House of Representatives of the United States of America in Congress assembled:

SEC. 1. That the right of way through the public lands be, and the same is hereby granted to the Great Southern Railroad Company, a corporation created under the laws of the state of Florida, its successors and assigns, for the construction of a railroad and telegraph from the Saint Mary's River, in the State of Florida, to Key West, in said State, together with a branch from the most eligible point on said road to Tampa Bay and Caloosa Entrance in said State, and the right, power and authority are hereby given to said corporation to take from the public lands adjacent to said road materials for the construction thereof. Said right of way is granted to said railroad to the extent of one hundred feet in width on each side of the central line of said road where it may pass through the public domain, including grounds for stations, buildings, work shops, depots, machine shops, switches, side tracks, turn tables and water stations, to an amount not exceding twenty acres for each ten miles, in length of said railroad : *Provided,* That one year from the passage of this act the said company shall file with the Secretary of the Interior, its acceptance of the terms of this act, and a map of the route exhibiting the line of the road and its branches as the same has been located, and shall complete said road within ten years of the passage of the act.

It shall be the duty of said company to permit any other railroad which has been or shall be authorized by the United States, or of the said State of Florida, to form running connections with its road, on fair and equitable terms. In case of disagreement, such terms shall be fixed by the Secretary of the Interior.

SEC. 2. That said road shall be a post route and military road, and Congress at any time, having due regard to the rights of said company, may fix rates of tariff for the transportation of troops, munitions of war, and mails, and may add to, alter, or amend this act.

SEC. 3. That Congress reserves to itself the right to alter, amend, or repeal this act whenever in its judgment the interests of the people may demand it.

Approved June 4, 1872.

> DEPARTMENT OF THE INTERIOR, }
> WASHINGTON, D. C., 31st May, 1873. }

SIR:

I have received your letter of the 24th ultimo, with the accompanying certified copy of the records of the Great Southern Railway Company, accepting the terms of the act of Congress, approved 4th June, 1872 (17 Statutes, 224), entitled "An Act granting the right of way through the public lands for the construction of a railroad and telegraph in Florida," and also with a map of the route, exhibiting the line of the road and its branches as the same has been located. This acceptance and this map are filed in accordance with the requirements of the first section of the said act.

I am, sir, very respectfully,

Your obt. servant,

C. DELANO, Secretary.

M. H. ALBERGER, Esq.
  Secretary of Great Southern R'w. Co.,
    Jacksonville, Florida.

CONSOLIDATION.

On the 10th day of November, 1874, in accordance with the power granted by the 11th section, of the charter of the Great Southern Railway Company of Georgia; and by the power granted by an Act, supplementary to the charter of the Great Southern Railway Company of Florida; the two companies were consolidated, under the name and title of the GREAT SOUTHERN RAILWAY COMPANY (CONSOLIDATED.)

THE LOCATION OF THE GREAT SOUTHERN RAILWAY.

The line of this railway as located, and partly constructed, commences at Millen, Georgia, connecting there with the Central Railroad of Georgia, and thence running in as near an air line south, as the nature of the country will admit, passing through Jesup, Georgia, and King's Ferry on the Georgia and Florida line, and thence, in Florida, through Jacksonville, Palatka, and Orlando; thence bearing east sufficiently to pass the Everglades, and following the Hunting Grounds to Turtle Harbor; thence passing to Key Largo and following the line of the Florida Keys to Key West—a length of main line of 720 miles; a branch road commencing at Palatka and passing by Dade Massacre Field to Tampa Bay and the Gulf of Mexico, midway of the west coast of the peninsula of Florida, a length of the branch line of 126 miles.

The company expects to operate its own steamers from the

southern terminus of the road to all the principal ports of the West Indies, Central America and South America.

CHARACTER OF THE ROUTE.

The three following reports, by Engineers Smith, Williams and Bailey, and the letter of ex-Senator Mallory, descriptive of the Florida Keys, give a very clear and comprehensive description of the route over which the line of the road runs from Jesup, Georgia, to Key West, Florida.

The route from Millen to Jesup, Georgia, 70 miles, is through a high, open pine country, with but one river of importance, the Altamaha, to cross.

LOCATION OF THE ROAD BETWEEN JESUP, GEORGIA, AND JACKSONVILLE, FLORIDA.

Engineer C. F. Smith, in his report of the location of the road between Jesup, Georgia, and Jacksonville, Florida, says: " Without entering into details, it will suffice for the present to give the general character of the line as located, particularizing only those points where change in configurations would seem to require a more defined description.

The line beginning at Jesup, where it makes connection with the Atlantic and Gulf, and the Macon and Brunswick railroads, pursues a southerly direction, crossing a tributary of the Finhalloway, near its junction with the main stream, thus avoiding an extensive trestle over the Finhalloway. After slightly curving eastward, passing the head of the Finhalloway, a slight deflection westward brings the line in correct position, passing over the most favorable ground to the Brunswick and Albany railroad, about midway between Waynesville and the Satilla river, thence with slight deflections (its general course being direct), it reaches the Satilla river at

Owens Ferry. Crossing the river at this point, and encountering the rice fields of Duncan Clinch, Esq., a curve to the east is made to reach the hard land, thereby avoiding a long and costly trestle. After making a curve southward, the line is brought in proper direction, crossing over a favorable surface to reach the St. Mary's River at King's Ferry. After crossing this river, a slight curve is made westward, thence the line pursues a south course to a point near Callahan, where a curve to the east is made, which gives a favorable direction to the line for crossing the Florida Railroad at Callahan, and continuing it to a point about one mile north of Thomas Creek, where a small curve westward gives direction to the line, reaching the Jacksonville, Pensacola and Mobile Railroad, at a point six miles west of Jacksonville, making the entire distance from the Atlantic and Gulf, and Macon and Brunswick Railroads at Jesup, to the Jacksonville, Pensacola and Mobile Railroad, ninety and twelve-one hundredths (90 $\frac{12}{100}$) miles.

The surface of the country over which the line passes, is extremely favorable for railroad construction, necessitating no gradients exceeding forty (40) feet in a mile, and this only in a few instances and for very short distances, no engineering difficulties which are not easily surmounted, (the principal of which are the rivers above mentioned), are encountered through the portion of the route herein reported upon. These are the only points requiring structures of greater magnitude than the ordinary structures of railroads, having sufficient capacity to pass the accumulated drainage during a wet season.

FROM SAINT MARY'S RIVER TO TURTLE HARBOR.

CHARACTER OF THE ROUTE.—The St. Mary's river at King's

ferry is deep, admitting vessels of EIGHTEEN FEET DRAFT FROM THE ATLANTIC to that point. It is about 350 feet wide, with high banks, which are not subject to overflow.

From King's ferry to Jacksonville, *via* Callahan, on the Florida Railroad, the projected line of road passes through flat pine land, interspersed with cypress ponds. This land is valuable for cultivation, and the greater portion well timbered with large and valuable pine timber. There are three small creeks to cross, but the crossing is not. at all expensive. Upon this section no deep cuts or high embankments will be required, and no grade greater than 20 feet per mile. .

From Jacksonville to Middleburg the country is very much of the same character, although the pine timber upon this section has been to a great extent cut off, for the reason that the line of railroad passes so near the navigable waters of the St. John's river, giving facilities for rafting timber. There are some small creeks to cross, but none of them requiring any expensive work.

Middleburg is situated upon Black Creek, a navigable river, about 250 feet wide, with high banks, which never overflow. From this point to the Bellamy road, west of Picolata, the country is slightly more rolling than the two sections previously described. For the most part, the pine land is good and excellently timbered. There are several small branches running into Black Creek, to cross, but a single span of trestle will cross them. The whole of the land, on the line from Middleburg to the Bellamy road, and I may say to Palatka, would be in great demand for the valuable timber upon it, if this railroad was in operation. From the Bellamy road to Palatka the country is very level, with two creeks to cross, each of them about 30 feet wide, with bluff banks.

From Palatka to Orange Springs the country is very level,

and the land well timbered ; there are two creeks to cross, but both of them small.

From Orange Springs to Adamsville the line passes through one of the best populated and most fertile regions of East Florida. It is slightly rolling, but requiring nowhere a higher grade than 60 feet per mile. There is much valuable land upon this portion of the line. There is not a stream to cross from Orange Springs, *via* Ocala, to Adamsville. The pine timber is particularly valuable.

From Adamsville the line passes near the foot of the chain of sand hills extending south from the Aha-popka Lake and runs through a flat pine and cypress pond country to Township 30 S., Range 27 E. At this point the line would strike the sand hills above mentioned, dividing the waters of the Kissimmee and Pease Creek. This sand ridge is about four miles wide, but can be easily crossed with a grade of not more than 40 feet per mile, and without expensive excavations or embankments. After crossing this ridge, the line strikes the flat land on the Kissimmee, and the country is almost a perfect level the balance of the entire route to Turtle Harbor. The pine timber from these sand hills South is not so good, but there is a large quantity of live oak upon the hammocks upon the edges of the prairies and savannas along the Kissimmee river. There is also a large quantity of this prairie and savanna land exceedingly valuable for cultivation, and particularly the cultivation of sugar.

The line, after crossing the Kissimmee, which is a river about 150 feet wide, until it reaches Township 36 S., Range 35 E., would be through the prairies of the Kissimmee. The road-bed would be firm, but perhaps it would require to be thrown up 12 inches. The earth from the side ditches would be sufficient.

From Township 36 S., Range 35 E., *via* Forts Loyd and, Van Swearingen, the line runs upon a slightly elevated ridge, dividing the waters of the Okeechobee Lake and the Haipahttokee and St. Lucie river, until it reaches Township 40 S., Range 41 E. There is a large quantity of saw-grass land, the best soil I ever saw, lying East of this ridge, and draining into the above last named rivers, which, with comparatively little cost, could be put into cultivation. There are also many small live oak hammocks in and upon this saw-grass land.

From Township 40 S., Range 41 E., to the Miami river, the line runs on a narrow strip or ridge of pine land lying between the Everglades and the inlets and bays of the Atlantic.

As I said before, the country is level, and well adapted to the construction of a railroad—the Hillsboro River, Middle River, New River, Snake Creek, Arch Creek, Little River, and the Miami River to cross. But none of these streams will require a trestle more than 200 feet long. Along this line, and upon the rivers and the Atlantic coast, will be, upon the completion of this road, the most attractive country in the South for the cultivation of tropical fruits, coffee, &c., as well as the point of attraction to the very large number of visitors from more Northern climes to enjoy a tropical winter.

The same narrow ridge of pine land above referred to extremely rocky, of coral formation, but almost perfectly level, continues to Turtle Harbor. All of this ridge is the best tropical fruit country in the United States.

There are, from Fort Van Swearingen, in Township 37 S. Range 37 E., to Turtle Harbor, hundreds of hammocks of the richest land known to our portion of the United States. These hammocks have a large growth of live oak, with other growth unknown elsewhere in Florida. There are also upon this division large bodies of savanna and saw-grass lands (and there can be no lands richer) which could be cheaply put into cultivation.

  * The route laid down passes many of the most beautiful inland lakes to be found in the world, and the lands are of great value. Every acre of them would have been in cultivation before the war but for their isolation and great distance from communication. Upon no other line of railroad in the United States can a country be reached so rich in its resource for tropical productions, and the value of its pine forest.

Very Respectfully,

M. A. WILLIAMS,
Civil Engineer.

AVAILABILITY OF TURTLE HARBOR.

Turtle Harbor can be entered with 27 feet at all times by steam vessels, and sailing vessels can ride safely at anchor in the outer harbor, until opportunity serves to enter the inner harbor. Depots can be built without difficulty.   *   *   *

The great superiority of Turtle Harbor as a *harbor* is thus manifest.   *   *   *   *   *   *

Very respectfully yours,

J. E. HILGARD,
In charge of Coast Survey Office.

ADAPTATION OF THE FLORIDA KEYS FOR THE LOCATION AND CONSTRUCTION OF A RAILROAD.

Mr. Bailey, civil engineer, and Chief Engineer of the International Oceanic Telegraph Company at the time of the construction of that line, surveyed the route for the railway from Biscayne Bay to Key West, along the line of the Keys.

His report shows that the road can be constructed from Biscayne Bay to Key West, at a slight cost per mile above ordinary railroad construction, and for less money than roads average in the cost of construction in New England.

——— ———

LETTER FROM HON. STEPHEN R. MALLORY.

Mr. Mallory was a native of Key West, where he resided till middle life, and was fully conversant with the subject of which he treats. In this we have the practical opinion of a native of Florida, and one who knows well that whereof he speaks. It shows that a gentleman who was once Chairman of the Naval Committee, Senate of the United States, and afterwards Secretary of the Confederate Navy, has published the very best argument for maintaining the maritime supromacy of the United States in its own waters, of connecting its trade throughout its whole territory, and of connecting its principal cities with the most productive country of the continent by the shortest and safest route. The letter is as follows :

KEY WEST, FLORIDA, May 28, 1871.

MY DEAR SIR :

* * * The practicability of constructing a railroad from this place to Key Biscayne Bay and thence to a junction with existing railroads of the country, is evident to all who have bestowed attention upon the subject, and its accomplishment would materially shorten the sea travel ; but the question whether existing interests, directly and indirectly involved in its construction, justify the enterprise, is one upon which men may well differ.

Col. Heiss, the able and energetic Superintendent of the International Telegraph Company, has recently completed a *reconnoissance* of the country along the Atlantic Sea Board, from Jacksonville, on the Saint John's River, to the Hunting Grounds, at the Western extremity of Key Biscayne Bay; and from his report we may safely assume that the entire route between these points is especially favorable to railroad construction, and that it presents no greater obstacles than those surmounted in building the Fronandina and Cedar Key Road. It is well timbered with heavy pine, and well watered, of a uniform elevation above tide water, and the lands generally invite cultivation. Key Biscayne Bay, about six by ten miles in extent, is a beautiful sheet of water, and the Miami and Little River and other smaller streams all flowing from the Everglades whose Southern edge—six feet above tide water—is but five miles from the Bay, flow into it. Settlements have existed on this Bay for a century past continuously, and at present it is attracting the attention of parties wishing to cultivate tropical fruits.

A Railroad Practicable to Key West.—From the main land from the Western extremity of this Bay, the distance to Key West is 130 nautical miles; and an air line between these points would pass over keys which, like beads upon a string, link this island with the main land of South Florida. The cuts or passes between them are generally shallow and narrow and there is but one where nine feet of water can be found. They are all above the influences of the sea, and are, with few exceptions, densely covered with timber and a soil susceptible of cultivation. The theory that tropical fruits attain their greatest perfection nearest their northern limit finds its verification here, where the lemon, the lime, the pine apple, the sugar-apple, the sour sop, the sapadella, plantain and bannana, are superior to the same fruits of Cuba, and that of the West Indies generally, as is the orange of

3

Louisiana and Florida to that of the more southern latitudes. The agave sisilliana from which the campeche or siral hemp is manufactured, must soon become an important staple here. It flourishes as does the saw palmetto of the South or black jack scrub of West Florida, without care or cultivation, and is as equally defiant of all enemies. A good machine for cleaning it is all that is necessary to induce the immediate occupation of all the keys for its production. Many of them possess fine ,salt ponds, capable of producing millions of bushels, when in very dry seasons a superior salt is spontaneously produced and these will all be utilized under the influence of the suggested railroad.

Could you visit this region, and there are few portions of our country more attractive in winter, you would, I think, recognize the extraordinary advantages of a railroad to Key West, whose capacious harbor the largest ships of war or commerce may safely enter by day or night.

As your chart of this coast may not properly present the chain of islands referred to as lying under an air-line of Key Biscayne Bay to Key West, I will state them from personal observation and a memory tolerably reliable : Beginning at the Bay, we have the Ragged Keys, Soldier Keys, Elliott's Key, Old Rhodes' Key, Key Largo (thirty miles long), Upper Mata Coomba, Lower Mata Coomba, Long Key, · Conch Keys, Grassy Keys, Duck 'Key, Krall Key, Vacas Keys, Knights Key, Pine Keys (the only Keys with pine barrens), Pigeon Key, Molasses Keys, Bahia Honda Keys, Sumerlin Keys, Sugar-loaf Key, New Found Harbor Key, Saddle Hill Keys, Boca Chica Keys, and Key West.

There are hundreds of other islands of like character lying along the route and varying in extent from 10 to 1000 acres, and nowhere on the globe are fish and turtle found in greater abundance or perfection.

Without special knowledge upon the subject, and without the data at hand for greater accuracy, I can still designate many of the steamships now employed between Cuba and the United States, and which are maintained mainly by the transportation of passengers.

There are seventeen passenger steamers, to which your better information may add, employed between the United States and Cuba, and upon voyages varying in length from sixty hours (between New Orleans and Havana), to one hundred and thirty-two hours (between Havana and New York). The proposed railroad to connect Key West with existing roads in Florida, and thence with the railroad system of the United States, would at once reduce the sea voyage between Cuba and any of our cities to six hours, the distance between Havana and this island from wharf to wharf being ninety miles, and the time between New York and Havana would be reduced from 132 to 80 hours.* From a candid consideration of the increase of travel which a reduction of ocean routes and of time, increased facilities and securities everywhere, indeed we are justified in assuming that the opening of this route would double the travel between Cuba and the United States in two years, a result in which every branch of industry and trade in our country is interested. I omit all reference to that immense travel which the completion of the Tehuantapec road and canal (with the Panama and other connections) must induce, and which would mainly pursue this route. At this moment proposals are invited for receiving at Key West from China across the Isthmus and forwarding hence to New Orleans a large number of emigrant coolies.

A survey of the route referred to demonstrate the practicability of constructing the road within the ordinary limits of expenditure per mile for railroad enterprises of our country. Not a yard of excavation would be required, and the character of the Islands insure the most substantial of road beds. Under certain conditions the teredo is, perhaps, more active and destructive in these waters than in any others under the American flag ; but these conditions could not exist along this route, where piling would be chiefly confined to very shallow depths. An examination of the piles of all the wharves here show that the teredo's greatest power is exercised upon the piles that stand in the deepest water and strongest currents, and almost exclusively on that part of the pile which the average highest and lowest tidal movement ; a space of about 26 inches.

Military Importance of the Road.—But there is a national view of this enterprise apart from the sale of public land, and consequent general development of paramount interest, and I will rather indicate it than state it in detail. In the event of a maritime war with a strong naval power, it is safe to assume that the first general naval action in which we shall be engaged, (assuming that we may have sea-going iron-clads) will be here in the strait of Florida ; the actual mouth of the Mississippi. The Gulf of Mexico is, in form, a demijohn on its side, its neck or outlet formed by Cuba upon the South, and Florida upon the North. The distance between Key West and the Captain General's palace in Havana is but 90 miles, a distance which six ordinary steamers may bridge across and communicate with each other every 20 minutes. Nothing could pass even this small fleet unobserved. Through this narrow pass, this mouth not only of the gulf, but of the Mississippi, must come its vast and increasing commerce ; and consequently here, beyond all other places upon the deep, would a strong naval power find its most attractive objective point.

We have constructed large works at Tortugas, Fort Jefferson, and a heavy work at Key West, Fort Taylor, at a fabulous expense, in recognition of this truth; and for six or eight months past the harbor of Key West has bristled with monitors and other naval ships, whose presence has doubtless exercised a conservative influence upon even the conduct of Cuban affairs. Unless the location and construction of these forts be a farce and a failure, no man will deny the importance of securing the readiest means of reinforcing and relieving them. All supplies to them now, and the transportation of all troops to this point, are dependent on the risk of a sea voyage of days; whereas, with the railroad in question established, military and naval reinforcements and supplies would not only reach them without such risks, but would reach them in about one-fourth the time now employed. Is it not fair to assume, therefore, that in this national aspect, would our government regard this enterprise, and that, so regarding it, governmental assistance would advance its construction, with the approval of all political schools.

M.

THE ACCOMPANYING MAP.

Accompanying this statement is a map of the line of the GREAT SOUTHERN RAILWAY and its more noteworthy connections.

Charter and Corporate Rights for Ocean Steamers.—The company have not only chartered rights for the line of the road, but also corporate rights to own and operate ships propelled by steam, or other power, as an integral part of their line. The principal railroad connections with all parts of the United States, may be traced by the lines of existing railroads. The more important steamship connections which it is intended to make are traced. Each of these lines so traced will be remunerative as soon as the railroad is completed, and will to a great extent take the place of existing steamship lines from the several terminal points to New York and Europe; the *railroad superseding the necessity of the ocean transportation*, by its shorter and quicker lines of internal communication.

Distance saved.—To illustrate : we have 90 miles of ocean transportation from the railroads of Cuba to the railroad at Key West, and 1245 miles from the railroads of Cuba to the railroads of New York, and we find that Key West is nearer by railroad communication to Nashville than New York. San Francisco is nearer by railroad to Key West than it is to New York. Hence all freights and passengers to and from the West Indies, will follow this line, saving not only in railroad transportation, but 1,155 miles of ocean transportation, via New York, which city at present monopolizes the West India trade in this country. Care was taken in preparing the map to show these facts.

Panama Railroad.—The avenue of communication with West Coast of Mexico and South America, is now by the Panama Railroad. The map shows that by this line more than half the distance from New York to Aspinwall can be made by rail. A vast business, therefore, with the West Coast of America, will enter the United States by this line.

Darien Ship Canal.—The construction of the Ship Canal across the Isthmus of Darien in the near future is now placed beyond controversy. The United States Government has taken an interest in the.work, and the surveys made by the government demonstrate its feasibility. It now remains

only a question of time when this work will be commenced
and completed. It requires no second glance at the map to
convince one that this Railway will be the great through
line of communication for all the United States with this
work; and the transactions and communications of the
Government of the United States with the work, while in
process of construction, or subsequently, will be by this road,
The rapidity with which the people of the United States
transact business will make this road the main, and almost
the sole, means of communication with and through this
canal.   This cannot be questioned, when it is well known
that one thousand one hundred and fifty five miles of ocean
travel and transportation is avoided in direct communication
with New York City.

RAILROAD CONNECTIONS OF THE GREAT SOUTH-ERN RAILWAY.

This Railway constitutes a continuous line from Millen,
Georgia, there connecting with the north and south roads from
New York city terminating at Millen, which is half way from
New York city to Key West, the extreme Southern key of
Florida, and southernmost point of the United States. At
this point communication is secured with the Entire Railroad System of Cuba, by a ferriage of ninety miles across
the Strait. In other words, the present water communication
of 1,155 miles to New York is reduced to a day-light passage
of 90 miles; the remainder of the trip being on a north and
south railroad, and made in a small fraction of the time now
required. The beauty of the country and the salubrity of
the climate through which this line passes is more fully mentioned elsewhere, as well as the vast commerce and wealth
that is tributary to the road, from the Peninsula of Florida,

from Cuba, from all the other West India Islands, from Central America, and from South America. It can have no competition, and by the laws of commerce, must be financially successful.

It is the most Important National Work now in Progress in the United States.—The military, naval and postal value of the work, elsewhere alluded to, cannot be over-estimated. In these departments the government will largely patronize the road in time of peace, and in time of war or threatening hostilities with any naval power, the government will save millions of dollars in rapidity of transportation and safe inland communication to the Keys, the naval and military stations at Key West and the Tortugas and the passage to the Gulf, and have the military and naval depots always accessible and always protected.

Railroad Connections. — Too much attention cannot be given to the advantageous location of the road relative to all other roads which it crosses, or with which it connects. Had every one of the eight roads with which it has immediate connections been constructed originally with the view of being made especially available for the benefit of this road, they could not have been more happily located.

Saint John's Railroad.—Commencing with the most southern of the roads tributary to this one in Florida, we have the Saint John's Railway, from St. Augustine (the oldest city in the United States, and a famous watering place), to Tocoi. The road is completed, is sixteen miles in length, and can make connection with no railroad but this.

Jacksonville, Pensacola and Mobile Railroad.—The next road north is the Jacksonville, Pensacola and Mobile Railroad. It is crossed by this railway at its eastern terminus, Jacksonville. This road is now completed and in operation to Chattahoochie, 250 miles. When completed it will be the most southern, east and west trunk line, nearest the Gulf coast, and by existing lines and those in process of construction, continuous to the Pacific coast.

Florida Railroad.—The next road still to the north is the Florida road, 156 miles in length, and is completed. This road runs northeast and southwest across the Peninsula of Florida, from the port of Fernandina on the Atlantic Ocean to the port of Cedar Key on the Gulf of Mexico. The line of this railway crosses the Florida road at Callahan, twenty-five miles from Fernandina, and is the only outlet for the Florida road to the North. Indeed the location of the Florida road is such that it must necessarily throw almost its entire business upon this, and become practically a completed extension or branch of it, 156 miles in length, with two good ports, one on the Atlantic Ocean and one on the Gulf of Mexico.

Brunswick and Albany Railroad.—The next road to the north is the Brunswick and Albany Railroad, already completed 240 miles from Brunswick, a magnificent harbor on the Atlantic coast of Georgia, to Albany. The continuation of this line to a connection with the railroads in central Alabama is now in progress. This road, being an East and West road, will be tributary in a large degree, by carrying freight and passengers from the East and West to this road, for southern market or travel. It will also be one of the main lines to receive freight and passengers from the South, for central Georgia, Alabama, Mississippi and the west. The Brunswick and Albany will in every way be advantageous to this road, as regards both passengers and freights.

JESUP.—The next railroad crossing still to the north is at Jesup. Here this Railway crosses two railroads—the Atl intic and Gulf and the Macon and Brunswick—at their present crossing, thus bringing the three roads together at Jesup, the most flourishing town in Southeastern Georgia.

Atlantic and Gulf Railroad.—The Atlantic and Gulf Railroad, running from Savannah, on the Savannah River, to Bainbridge and Albany, in Southwestern Georgia, a completed road three hundred and forty-four miles in length, traverses the State of Georgia in a Northeast and Southwest course, and will be tributary in passengers and freight from Savannah to Florida and vice versa. The line of this road, southwest of Jesup, will in the same manner, and to a large extent, be tributary to that portion of this road north of Jesup in all direct travel and traffic with all the States north of that point. The distance saved over the present route, via Savannah to Millen, is one hundred and fifty miles. Thus the location of the line of this Railway diagonally across the Atlantic and Gulf Railroad, makes the latter road northeast of Jesup one of its principal patrons in the commerce of the through line south, while that portion southwest of Jesup becomes one of its chief patrons for the commerce north.

Macon and Brunswick Railroad.—The Macon and Brunswick Railroad, crossing the Atlantic and Gulf Railroad and Railway at Jesup, is a completed road in operation, commencing at the Port of Brunswick, on the Atlantic coast of Georgia, and those running Northwest to Macon 195 miles. This road is a first-class tributary to this Railway, indeed as much so as the Florida road. All travel of passengers and all transportation of freight from the portions of the road east of Jesup, bound north to the city of New York and elsewhere in the Northern and Eastern States, will take this Railway north of Jesup, it being a saving to Millen and the North, of 150 miles.

The portion of the Macon and Brunswick Road west of Jesup operates as a branch of this Railway, it being the shortest line from the South to the Northwest, the connections by this line being perfect, and on an air line to the Northwestern States. Cars by this line can be run from Key West to the cities of Nashville, Louisville, Memphis, Cincinnati, Saint Louis, Chicago, and all other cities of the West, without breaking bulk, and on the shortest line. The value of the connection, and the facilities thus offered, cannot be overestimated when we consider the vast quantities of tropical fruits from Florida, the West Indies and South America which will seek the markets of the North and West over these lines of quick transportation, and with little handling, to reach a market with so perishable freight, all travel of passengers and transportation of freight from all the Northwestern States to the Peninsula of Florida, and to the West Indies and South America, will use this line, it being by far the shortest and most convenient.

It is mainly on this line that the heavy freights from the tropics will leave this Railway for the Northwest. By reference to the map, it will be seen that the shortest railroad communication to all the Northwestern and Western States, by which Sugar, Molasses, Coffee, Indigo, Spices, Cocoa, Fruits, and numberless other tropical products, can be transported is by this Railway and the Macon and Brunswick Railroad and its connecting lines. By this line the freights from Cuba and the other Southern countries are as near Tennessee, Kentucky, and all the States to the West and Northwest of these, before they leave Havana, as they are at New York, after the expense of 1,300 miles of ocean transportation, the handling and storage in New York.

The same statement holds good for different sections of

the country, via the Jacksonville, Pensacola and Mobile Railroad, by the Brunswick and Albany Road, and especially so via the Millen and Augusta branch of the Central Railroad of Georgia, over which the States of South Carolina, North Carolina, Virginia and West Virginia will be supplied with freights from the tropics.

Central Railroad of Georgia.—The next Railroad still North of Jesup with which this Railway connects is the Central Railroad of Georgia, at Millen, the Northern terminus of the Great Southern. The Central Railroad of Georgia is a completed road 541 miles in length, from Savannah to Macon, with a branch from Millen to Augusta, and with other branches and extensions under the same ownership. This road to the West gives an outlet for all of the Northern Georgia, Alabama and Tennessee. The many large cities of the Central States are brought into close and direct communication with the tropics by the Western extension of the Central Railroad of Georgia and this Railway, by the shortest line of transportation.

Augusta Branch of the Central Railroad of Georgia.—But of all the roads yet mentioned, the branch of the Central Railroad of Georgia, from Millen to Augusta, is of greatest importance to this Railway. It runs due North, from Millen to Augusta, 53 miles, and there unites with all the north and South Railroads between the Blue Ridge Mountains and the Atlantic Ocean. There are thus made complete north and south connections with the States of South Carolina, North Carolina, Virginia, West Virginia, Pennsylvania, Maryland, Delaware, New Jersey, New York, the New England States and the Canadas. By this complete connection all these States, the large cities and the 20,000,000 people in them, are brought into the closest possible communication with the West Indies and the tropics. Passengers can pass from the extreme north to the extreme south without weariness. The most delicate of tropical fruits and the productions of tropical Florida and the West Indies can be taken to the north by the most rapid transit. The immense losses now incurred by decay on the long ocean voyage will be avoided. Vast quantities of vegetables and fruits are now grown in Virginia and North and South Carolina in advance of the season at the North and delivered in northern markets in March and April, and upon the opening of this line they will be grown in still greater quantities in Florida and Cuba, and delivered in New York in December, January and February. The fruits of the tropics will be nearly as frequent in the northern markets and upon the table of every family as the fruits of northern productions are now. The season of garden vegetables and fruits, instead of being as now confined to the summer and autumn, will extend over the whole year, and instead of being confined to the productions of the north, will cover as well the productions of the tropics. No part of Europe has such facilities for bringing the productions of the temperate and torrid zone together, fresh in our market, as this road will give to the people of this country.

Other Advantages of these Railroad Connections.—The unprecedented facilities this railway, with its favorable connections, offers to the passenger travel cannot be too minutely investigated. The people continually passing south and north in the United States will find by this line all that can be desired to reach the southern limit of this country, and the greatest convenience to pass into the West Indies and South America and *vice versa*. The climate of the peninsula of Florida does now, and must always, offer to persons suffering with pulmonary diseases the best asylum in the world. The climate, for salubrity and healthfulness, surpasses that of Italy, and the scenery is no less agreeable and fascinating.

This railway, by reason of the directness of its line, the rapidity of transit by it, and its most remarkable and advantageous railroad connections, will secure over its 720 miles of road all express matter and fast freights. No combination of capitalists or of corporations can change this practically, for the peninsula of Florida can be traversed by no other . road.

———

CUBA, THE OTHER WEST INDIA ISLANDS, SOUTH AMERICA AND CENTRAL AMERICA.

The island of Cuba contains 1,800,000 people; the West India islands together about 5,000,000. Eleven per cent. of the entire commerce of the United States is with the West Indies. Central and South America are also in a great measure tributary to this railway, by reason of this being the shortest water communication to reach the railroad system of the United States. These countries together contain 44,000,000 of people. From these sources—the West Indies, South America and Central America—the United States has more than twenty per cent. of its entire commerce. In all this traffic no railroad can compete.

General Resources for Through Freights and Passengers.— With these resources of half a continent tributary to this road from the South, we have connections on the line itself with eight railroads, none of which could have been more advantageously located for branches and feeders. By these several roads we have complete railroad connections with every part of the United States and Canada, and will draw from the 'commerce of every State in the Union, and will carry the passengers and freight down one only trunk line of railroad of 720 miles to the straits of Florida. Cars may be loaded at any point in the United States, and without breaking bulk and without delay, be run to and over the entire length of this railway to the door of Havana, the mart of the West Indies, and to the gateway of South America. If it were possible that so long a road as this could be constructed and made dependent upon the patronage of other railroads alone and upon through traffic of fast freights and passengers, no line in America could equal this. The freights and passengers that must of necessity be thrown upon it from other roads will make it one of the best lines in America.

RIVERS TRIBUTARY TO THE GREAT SOUTHERN RAILROAD.

Besides the many connections this road will have with other railroads, it has valuable connections in crossing the several navigable rivers which run perpendicular to the line of the road, and which will bring to it large amounts of cotton, of general freights, and immense amounts of lumber.

Altamaha, Oconee and Ocmulgee.—The most northern of these rivers is the Altamaha, which is crossed by the road eighty miles below Millen, and one hundred miles from the mouth of the river. The Altamaha is formed by the junction of Oconee and Ocmulgee. There are thirteen feet of water over the bar of the river at ebb-tide. The junction of the Oconee and Ocmulgee is about one hundred miles above the railroad crossing. The Oconee is navigable to Milledgeville, and the Ocmulgee to Macon. There are six hundred miles of the navigable waters of the Altamaha and its tributaries above the crossing of the road. The banks of the Altamaha, the Ocmulgee, and the Oconee, are covered the entire length, either with cotton plantations, or by the finest yellow pine and cypress forests in the world. This north and south road will secure more of the traffic of these rivers than any other.

Satilla.—The next considerable navigable river south of the Altamaha is the Satilla or Saint Illa river, fifty miles south of the Altamaha. The road crosses this river forty miles from the ocean. The course is through a rich and well-timbered country. Many valuable and highly cultivated Sea Island Cotton and rice plantations are on it. These are very productive, and the cotton and rice produced is of the finest quality. There are many extensive lumber mills on the river. The road crosses at Owen's Ferry. The entire length on each bank, not occupied by plantations, is covered with splendid yellow pine and other timber, most valuable for building and manufacturing purposes.

Saint Mary's.—The next considerable river on the south is the Saint Mary's—the boundary line between Georgia and Florida. The road crosses at King's Ferry thirty miles from its mouth. The depth of water on the bar admits the passage of ships drawing twenty feet. The river has an excellent channel, with sixteen feet of water to Trader's Hill, thirty miles above the railroad crossing, and twelve feet fifty miles higher. The collection ports of Saint Mary's, Georgia, and Fernandina, Florida, are both on this river, and are fine towns and of large business interests. The town of Coleraine, near the railroad crossing, is a fine village. Trader's Hill, at the head of navigation, is a thriving village. The lumber and timber business are very extensive. The banks of the Saint Mary's are high and the country beautiful.

Business to the Road.—The business accruing to the road

from the Altamaha, Satilla and the Saint Mary's rivers will be large. The road in this business has, and can have, no rival.

Other Rivers.—Thus far, only three of the Georgia rivers have been mentioned. There are others such as the Osgeecheo and Cannouchee, that are available for lumber purposes. Hundreds of vessels each year load with lumber at Georgia ports for foreign countries.

Saint John's River.—Thirty miles south of the Saint Mary's the road touches the Saint John's river, at Jacksonville. This city is a port of entry, has 20,000 inhabitants, and in business and enterprise has no superior in the country. The Saint John's river runs due north, and enters the ocean twenty-five miles from Jacksonville. South of Jacksonville it has, with its tributaries, more than 600 miles of navigable waters, and a rapidly increasing population on its banks. It traverses the most delightful country and climate in America. This road connects the Saint John's river, and all the country tributary thereto, by an air line, with the Northern and Northwestern States and is one of the largest lumbering towns in the South.

REPORT OF SENATE COMMITTEE.

The Company asked of Congress a grant of land in aid of that portion of the line in Florida.

The following is from the Report of the Committee.

IN THE SENATE OF THE UNITED STATES.

(June 13, 1870.)

The Committee on Public Lands made the following.

REPORT.

[To accompany Bill S. No. 438.]

The charter of the Great Southern Railway Co. was granted by the Legislature of the State of Florida in February, at

4!

which time the company perfected their organization. The charter authorizes the construction of a railroad from the Saint Mary's River, on the Georgia and Florida line, beginning about forty miles from the Atlantic coast and running south to the city of Jacksonville, and thence south to Biscayne Bay, near Cape Florida, the most southern harbor in the United States.

The length of the road will be four hundred and twenty miles. There are upon the line of this road tracts of land that cannot be made available for agricultural purposes; but there is much, perhaps two-thirds, that is susceptible of cultivation for sugar, cotton and the semi-tropical and tropical fruits, if communication and transportation can be made through it. Wherever transportation is now available the productions of the country are exceedingly profitable, being those which cannot be produced elsewhere in the United States.

Large tracts of country, even whole counties, which now are devoted only to pasturing, are susceptible of producing sugar, cotton and all the fruits of the tropics, in the greatest abundance and with great profit.

The charter of this corporation provides that the company may own and operate, in connection with their road, both steam and sailing vessels as an integral part of their franchise. The officers of the corporation represent the intention and object to the company to be that of establishing a thorough and quick line of passengers and freight transportation with all the West India Islands, but more especially with Cuba, Porto Rico, Jamaica, Hayti and San Domingo. They represent that, after long, careful study and much patient research, they are confident that the road will be of inestimable value and benefit, not only to the State but to the country at large, and will, in case of war, be of great value for the transportation of troops, supplies, munitions, &c., which is provided for in this bill, as also for the transportation of the mails it will be of especial value.

The distance that will be saved, in water transportation from Havana or any other of the West India ports, by the building of this road, will be five hundred miles over any other railroad connections. The distance from Biscayne to Matanzas is a trifle less than one hundred miles, and to Havana a trifle more, at either of which places connection is made with the Cuban Railroads. This makes comparatively but a ferry between the United States and Cuba. The advantages of connection will be shared the same with all the Islands. It will take from seven to ten hours only, by water, to cross between the United States and Cuba.

A few figures, in round numbers, as to the comparative wealth of Cuba and California, (to which we have just built a road, and are preparing to build another,) may not be out of place, to show how valuable to the country this proposed road will become, and to the company, if skillfully operated.

	Cal., 1860.	Cuba, 1860.
Population	379,994	1,359,238
Real and Personal Property	207,000,000	1,325,000,000
Agricultural Products	46,000,000	130,000,000

The commerce of Cuba was $144,000,000, of which the United States got $54,000,000. The relative valuation of property and commerce with Porto Rico and the other islands is about the same.

The officers of the company believe that, with the proper Railroad facilities, much more of the commerce of the West Indies will be controlled by the United States, and, indeed, in a few years, with this road and its steamship connections, the United States will control this commerce; the peninsula of Florida will be settled by an active and industrious people, and from the peculiar character of its climate, soil and productions, made one of the most flourishing portions of our country.

The committee are assured that the company is fully organized, and the preliminary arrangements for proceeding with the work have been made, and the work will be commenced and prosecuted with the greatest possible expedition as soon the lands asked for may be assured them.

The committee have carefully inquired into the whole matter, and are satisfied the purpose to build the road is good, and from the national character of the work, are of the opinion it demands more than the average attention given to bills granting lands to aid in the construction of railroads.

The committee have carefully considered the Bill, and recommend its passage.

TRANSPORTATION OF LUMBER.

The supply of valuable timber along the entire line of the Great Southern Railway is inexhaustible. Seven-tenths of the line in Georgia is through a virgin forest of the most magnificent yellow pine in the world. The timber is large, high, and of the finest quality. It is fitted, by its size, growth and quality, for masts, spars, square timber, timber for ship-building, house-building, cabinet ware, and indeed for all purposes for which the finest quality of yellow pine can be used.

Value of Timber.—One cannot conceive, unless familiarly acquainted with the country, how extensive and how valuable the timber of the Georgia and Florida pine forest is, wherever lines of transportation are opened and it is made available. Thousands of millions of feet may be cut and taken from along the line of this railway, either in Georgia or Florida, and no material diminution of the vast forests be seen or the supply materially reduced.

Permanency of Supply.—For a full century the lumber men have been drawing from the banks of the several rivers, and supplying the markets of Europe, the United States, the West Indies, Mexico and South America, with the masts, spars and yellow pine of Georgia and Florida. Yet even on these streams the supply is by no means exhausted. Indeed the cutting has advanced so far only as to make the expense of drawing logs to the streams by horse power too great while the great forests a short distance away from the river are left untouched.

Manufacture of Lumber and Timber.—The manufacture of hewn timber and lumber is extremely lucrative, and along the line of every railroad in Georgia, Florida and Alabama saw mills spring up as if by magic. All the railroads of these States are doing a large and lucrative business in the shipment of lumber to the ports of their several termini.

Profits accruing to Railroads.—But this is not all the profits of railroads accruing from the manufacture of lumber. Experience has shown that railroad transportation of logs, in taking them to the mills, is cheaper than transportation by horses, mules or oxen. On most of the roads in these States trains are run daily for the sole purpose of transporting logs to the mills and lumber to the seaboard.

Lumber Manufacture.—Several extensive mills are now established upon the line of this road, and a large proportion of the logs for this lumber is now carried over the Jacksonville Pensacola and Mobile road, or over short temporary railroads built by lumbermen for the sole purpose of transporting logs to these mills.

This road will open an entirely new field for this work, and a field which no man now living can see exhausted, but which each year grows more lucrative as the facilities become greater. Six hundred miles of this line of this road lies through this virgin pine forest.

Live Oak.—In the southern portion of Georgia the Live Oak forests are extensive; while in all the peninsula of Florida the Live Oak forests are the most extensive, and of the greatest value of any in the world.

So valuable are these forests that the Government has selected and reserved from sale large tracts of this live-oak land, for the exclusive use of the Navy.

These forests have been for the most part absolutely inaccessible. By this road they will be opened through their whole extent. Lumbermen will at once take advantage of this ready means of access, and quick transportation. The profits from this source will be large, and the advantage to the ship building interests, both of Europe and America, great.

Along the whole line of this Railway, there are many other valuable timbers which enter into all branches of mechanical industries in which woods of any kind are used—the cypress, red bay, palmetto, magnolia, and many other kinds of wood especially valuable for cabinet ware, and by this road they will be made available.

Profits of the Road from the Lumber Interests.—Experience has shown that many of the roads in the yellow pine districts of the South have paid, by the transportation of logs, timber and lumber, all the running and current expenses for their entire traffic.

No other road in all the country offers so great inducements in this branch of business. The magnificent forests through which it runs, the ability to carry either logs, timber or lumber to navigable waters at so many points, thus avoiding too great expense to the lumbermen, combine to make it certain that this road will be superior to any other in the speciality.

ESTIMATE OF THE VALUE OF YELLOW PINE LUMBER ON THE LINE OF THE ROAD.

A report of the War Department on the survey of the Choctawhatchie River, West Florida, Col. J. H. Simpson, U. S. Engineer, in charge, made to Congress, April 17, 1872, in estimating the resources of the country adjacent to the river, makes an estimate of the yellow pine timber, and the distance which logs can profitably be hauled, as three and a half miles, and the value of the timber at an average of forty five dollars per acre.

The line of the road runs through an unbroken yellow pine forest in every respect equal to that on the Choctawhatchie River, for more than six hundred miles. Estimating it at 600 miles there is a frontage on both sides of the road, of 1,200 miles. Three and a half miles on which timber may be drawn to the road on either side, gives 4,200 square miles, or 2,688,000 acres covered with yellow pine and available to the road. This 2,688,000 acres at forty five dollars per acre gives $120,960,000, as the value of the yellow pine available to this road.

Col. Simpson gives another estimate in which he states that the best authorities gives five miles at which timber may be profitably hauled. This would greatly increase the other estimate.

Extract from the Report of Charles F. Smith, Civil Engineer on that portion of the road [line between Jesup, Georgia, and Jacksonville, Florida.

The vast amount of business that out of necessity must grow out of the immense slope of timber in the yet untouched forests of the south, especially of Georgia and Florida is scarcely dreamed of even in the Northwest where the approaching timber famine is already inducing very serious apprehensions, concerning a supply for the present even, not to figure on a future, not far distant.

The importance of this single branch of trade as a source of revenue to the Great Southern Railway is no small item. Of the ninty-one miles between Jessup and Jacksonville, eighty-five miles is through a dense forest of yellow pine, with easy access by hauling with teams for three miles on either side, making 510 square miles or 360,400 acres of land lying adjacent to and along the line of the road, betweeen the points above named ; all of the logs and lumber from this land will necessarily find transit over the road.

At the very lowest estimate made by Mr. Smith, there is 816,000,000 feet, and at the present rates of freights on logs and lumber over this short space of the road, would amount to $4,080,000. Another thing which is not generally known in the North and Northwest, and which is a fact abundantly proven by very many years experience, that when these lands are once cleared of their large timber, the growth is so rapid that it replenishes itself to its full capacity of timber for sawing in fifteen years. Thus Mr. Smith says from this land alone an annual crop of lumber may be taken of 163,000,000 feet.

This is of especial importance by the growing scarcity of timber at the north and northwest, as the southern market will increase in an equal pace with the northern scarcity. A very large proportion of the yellow pine lumber of the south seeks a foreign market. The various connections of this road with the navigable waters of the Satilla, Saint Mary's and Saint

John's rivers which it crosses or touches, and the ports of Savannah, Brunswick and Fernandina, which are reached by short sections of railroads crossing this. These advantages in the shipment of logs and lumber very greatly enhance the value of this road, and of the timber itself by so easily carrying it to sea-going navigation.

———

STEAMSHIP TRANSPORTATION OF THE GREAT SOUTHERN RAILWAY.

The peculiar location of the road of this company, commencing as it does at Millen, near the northern boundary of Georgia, and midway between Canada and Key West, and thence running south, touching at Turtle Harbor to Key West, between 700 and 800 miles, will require the additional transportation of steam and sailing vessels. Key West is sixty miles south of the extreme southern point of the peninsula of Florida, and Turtle Harbor is on the southeast of the peninsula. A full development of the freight and passenger business of the road requires the continuance of the carriage by steamships south of the termini of the road, to all the ports of the West Indies, of the Caribbean Sea, Central and South America. Elsewhere we have shown the amount of this traffic that will pass over the road from tropical America, from the Panama Railroad and the Darien Canal, as soon as work on it has commenced. But this commerce must be gathered into Key West and Turtle Harbor by steamships and sailing vessels. The company has fully considered this question, and is fully aware of its importance and the necessity of establishing these lines of steamships.

The nation is now very deficient in steamship transportation on the waters south of the United States, and the entire force of steamers necessary to transact the business would need to be furnished by the company. To fully control the carrying trade intended to be reached, there will be required at least fifteen steamships ranging from 400 tons upwards. These vessels should be of iron and substantially built. Within two years after the line of road is opened, this number of vessels can be kept fully occupied. This will be more apparent when we consider that there are 107 steamships, registering 163,448 tons, plying regularly from European ports to the same ports that this company intends to reach, and which are now almost wholly or altogether neglected by the commerce of the United States.

From Turtle Harbor there will thus be established with the road, regular steamship connection with Nassau and other ports of the Bahama Islands, with Cardenas and other eastern ports of Cuba, the ports of Porto Rico, Hayti, San Domingo, and each one of the other West India Islands, to the east coast of Venezuela, the steamers on the Orinoco (owned by Americans), the ports of Dutch, French and British Guiana, all the ports of Brazil, the Amazon River, all the ports of Uruguay and the Argentine Republic.

From Key West there will be established connection by steamship with Havana and Matanzas, and at these ports making connection with the entire railroad system of Cuba, and receiving the enormous and valuable freights carried by them, the ports of Jamaica, of Southern Mexico, Yucatan, the Bolize, Nicaragua, Costa Rica, and the eastern terminus of the Panama Railroad; the ports of the United States of Columbia, the western ports of Venezuela, and by the Panama Railroad, with the whole western coast of Central and South America. In all more than 150 ports now having a fixed and established commerce. These ports range in the value of their imports and exports from sufficient only, to secure the establishment of communication, up to those ranking among the first 'ports in the world in the value of their commerce Such is the case with the cities of Havanna, Aspinwall, Rio Janerio, and Buenos Ayres.

It will be seen by reference to other parts of this pamphlet, how enormous is the preponderance of the commercial nations of Europe, over the United States, in the number and tonnage of vessels and the traffic carried by them. This too, applies both to the main land and the islands of tropical and semi-tropical America. The tonnage and traffic of Europe, in this commerce is so much greater than that of the United States, that the realization of it is humiliating to every comprehensive and well thinking American. The interchange in the production of the tropic and those of the temperate zones is almost beyond comprehension, and the successes in commerce and the habits of nations have made this inter-change a necessity of civilized life.

The enormous wealth of the mercantile nations of Europe, originally accrued to them, in a large degree, by their com-merce with the East Indies and other tropical countries of Asia. It has added to this the commerce of tropical America. The first they still monopolize, the latter nearly so. It will be noticed in the summary elsewhere given of the vessels trading between Europe and the West Indies, Central and South America, that only steamships are mentioned; while the sailing vessels engaged in the same traffic vastly exceed the steamship, in number, tonnage and carrying capacity.

The establishment of this road will call into its service many sailing vessels now unemployed or employed else-where. The southern termini of the road being just on the line between the temperate and torrid zones, will afford an opportunity not before existing on this continent for short and profitable trips for sailing vessels, in carrying perishable tropical fruits and other perishable productions of the South.

By the use of refrigerating cars, the most sensitive fruits grown in the tropics can be carried to any point in the North without injury or decay. The greater facilities of ingress, egress and anchorage afforded by the harbors of this road, superior to any harbor south of New York, will afford a great inducement for sailing vessels to engage in the service of the company.

There is another fact in connection with this enterprise that, in a national sense, should not be overlooked. We have shown elsewhere the directness and shortness of this line from the tropics to that portion of the United States north of the Apalachian mountains and west of the Alleghany mountains—that is, the valleys of the Ohio, the Northern Mississippi, and the Northern Lakes. This short line to the tropics would speedily make Chicago, Cleveland, Cincinnati, Louisville, St. Louis, Nashville, and many other cities the rivals of Boston, New York, Philadelphia, Baltimore and New Orleans in importing all the productions of the tropics, and surpass them in exporting the food products of the West to the tropics. Still further, it will cause the Great Basin of the West to become the rival of Europe in the commerce of the nations south of the United States. The construction of this road and its steamship connection is all that is now necessary to turn the commerce of tropical America from Europe to this country and give to the United States what in right belongs to it—the control of the commerce of this Continent. It never has had that control, and it is a duty it owes to itself to seize upon every advantage and secure to itself this commerce of hundreds of millions of dollars per annum. This road, with its ocean extensions, will rescue this commerce from Europe, and for all future time it will bo held by this country and by our own people. No public work has been projected, or can be, that will compare with this for controlling so vast a commerce. Indeed, the completion of this road, with its steamships added, will revolutionize the commerce of this Continent.

No one of the great national improvements recommended by the XLIII. Congress to bo undertaken and accomplished can be compared to this in improving the commerce of the country, or in increasing the material wealth of the people.

To the Company, as well as to the country, to the commerce and to the increasing wealth of the nation, resulting from the opening of this great trunk line of road as a route of transit for the commerce that will flow from the temperate to the torrid, and from the torrid to the temperate zone, the steamships to be placed in connection with the road, will be of as great importance as the road itself. The steamships will be an actual continuation of the road, to every considerable port south of the United States. It would be but a half completed work if the road was constructed without the addition of the steamships, or if the steamships were put on without the through line of road to rapidly carry the freights from the tropics to the interior of the United States, and *vice versa*. But combined the enterprise is complete and perfect. All that is claimed for the road will be accomplished speedily upon its completion. The hundreds of millions of dollars of the commerce of the nations south, that now finds it way direct to Europe will flow into this country and be controlled by it, and the people of the United States made richer by many_millions of dollars each year for all the future.

We need steamship lines to enable the people of South America, Central America and Cuba to communicate with us direct and to get the goods they buy direct. As it now stands a person from Rio Janeiro, desiring to buy goods in the New York market, would require to go to Liverpool and thence to New York. The consequence is he does not get to New York at all, but buys his goods in Liverpool. This is true of all South American ports. A steamship line is a great highway, and people will travel the road laid out for them.

England has always been keenly alive to this fact, and has subsidized steamship lines to any part of the earth where there has been even a remote chance of commerce resulting by such communication. But with us it is very different.

The steamship line is simply a continuation of the railroad, the one carrying from the seaboard what the other carries to it. It is of primary importance for our countrymen to see the fact, that if they wish the people of foreign countries to become our customers, and to buy here in preference to buying abroad, that they must open the way for them to come, and give them at least equal facilities of travel and transportation of freight, as they are furnished by England and other foreign countries, who are our direct competitors.

TRANSPORTATION OF COTTON.

The transportation of cotton will be a large item in the profits of the road. There were produced, as shown by the last census in the counties directly upon the line of the road or strictly tributary to it, 25,000 bales in.Georgia, and 40,000 bales in Florida. This cotton would seek a market over this road. But the main portion of the cotton transported by it will be that thrown upon it by the tributary roads. All the cotton from Florida, Southern and Southwestern Georgia,

sent direct to Charleston, Wilmington, Baltimore, Philadelphia, New York or Boston by rail, will pass over this
road, either from the Peninsula of Florida north, or from
Jesup, Ga., being there thrown upon it by the *Atlantic and
Gulf* road, by the *Brunswick and Albany* from the southwest,
and by the *Macon and Brunswick* road from the southeast
In the transportation of cotton to a market, a large portion of
it is sent over the shortest railroad lines, and in the quickest
time, and thus it would be given to this road.

Four-fifths of the country through which this railroad
passes is cotton producing country, and the opening of the
of the country by lines of communication will develop to an
unlimited extent the production of this staple.

Sea Island Cotton.—It is a fact wórthy of especial note that
the line of this railway traverses the full extent of the only
region in the world adapted to the culture of the Sea Island or
Long Staple Cotton. The only exception to this is a few
square miles of territory on the coast islands of South Carolina. This road enters the country producing Sea Island
Cotton exclusively, a few miles south of Jesup, and thence
south continues its entire length in the soil and climate peculiarly adapted to the production of this most valuable staple.
Short staple cotton is not grown at all upon the Peninsula of
Florida. The opening of this country by railroad will, in a
few years, quadruple the amount of Sea Island Cotton now
grown in the world. The cultivation of it has always been
lucrative, but the means of transportation from this, the only
large area adapted to its growth, have been wanting. The territory adjacent to the line of this road has an easy capacity of a
millions bales of long staple cotton, and if for no other reason
it should be opened to develop the growth of this most valuable product.

Letter from the Commissioner of Agriculture, transmitting, in answer to a Senate resolution of March 6, 1876, information in relation to the soil and climate adapted to the growth of sea island cotton.

DEPARTMENT OF AGRICULTURE, }
WASHINGTON, March 9, 1876. }

Sir :

Soil of marine formation appears to be necessary, and a sea atmosphere, with its warmth and equability. A sandy deposit of marine silt, but little above the sea level, permeable by the moisture beneath, and convenient for the requisite manuring by salt-marsh, furnishes conditions for the highest production of sea-island cotton.

Limited as is the area suited to the culture of this variety, it is by no means occupied. The economic aspects of this production have not been favorable to its extension. Among the largest crops produced are those of fifty years ago. The product of 1827 was fully 15,000,000 pounds, or 47,000 bales of 320 pounds each, while the average for the past ten years is less than half as much, or 7,000,000 pounds, nearly 22,000 bales. The record of these crops, with the geographical distribution of production, is as follows :

Years.	Florida.	Georgia.	South Carolina.	Texas.	Total.
1874............... bales	8,313	1,110	7,400	204	17,027
1873...............do	8,825	1,408	8,759	920	19,912
1872...............do	10,764	1,269	13,156	1,100	26,289
1871...............do	5,624	1,567	8,755	899	16,845
1870...............do	8,753	4,934	7,218	704	21,609
1869...............do	9,948	9,225	7,334	......	26,507
1868...............do	6,703	6,371	5,608	......	18,682
1867...............do	10,402	6,296	4,577	......	21,275
1866...............do	11,212	10,015	11,001	......	32,228
1865...............do	2,428	10,957	5,630	......	19,015
Total...............do.	82,972	53,152	79,438	3,827	219,389

Edisto Island, south of Charleston, is the most prominent locality for the production of long-staple cotton. Saint Simon's, Ukyl, and Skidoway are also favorably known for products of high quality.

In conclusion, the "geographical limits and area" in which sea-island cotton "matures perfect growth," include the islands of the coast of South Carolina, Georgia and Florida, and the Gulf of Mexico, and a few miles inland from the coast, ten or fifteen, more or less, the line extending farther inland up the river valleys which have a marine soil and unobstructed sea breeze, and encircling most of the area of Florida.

The proportion of upland to sea-island cotton product is about 200 to 1. Probably not more than 100,000 acres are now devoted to its culture, while that occupied in upland culture is from one hundred to one hundred and twenty times as much. The area could be increased immensely were conditions favorable—a sufficient price, more systematic and labor-saving modes of culture and preparation, and a more available and sufficient labor, the former residents of coasts and islands having gone to the cities, or retired to the uplands.

I am, yours very respectfully,

FRECK. WATTS,
Commissioner.

NAVAL STORES.

On every completed railroad in the yellow pine districts of the South the production and manufacture. of Naval Stores has become of great moment, and is everywhere lucrative. Very important improvements have been made in the process of manufacture of these stores, in consequence of which the business has already much increased, and is growing rapidly.

5

No locality in the world offers greater facilities for this branch
of industry than the line of this road. The very considerable
bulk of these stores will furnish the road with a large business, and enhance its profits. Many producers are now awaiting anxiously the opening of this road that they may open
the turpentine orchards along the line.

The extensive pine forests of Florida already furnish employment to a large number engaged in the production of
naval stores. The trees in Florida have a much longer running season than those of 'North or South Carolina. One
hand will take care of 12,000 boxes, which will yield 50 bbls.
of spirits of turpentine, and 200 bbls. of rosin, in a good
season. The business has been yearly increasing, and has
been remunerative.

Capt. C. F. Smith, civil engineer, says of that section of
the road between Jesup and Jacksonville: "The territory
along the ninety miles of this road is well timbered with yellow pine of excellent quality for the manufacture of naval
stores of all kinds. Notwithstanding the pressure of the
times, the manufacture of naval stores is now rapidly increasing along the line of the Florida railroads. New crops,
in some ten localities, are being opened along the Florida Railroad, and the results already form an important, even a leading feature, in the regular exports from Fernandina. The
land along the line of this railway is well adapted to the prosecution of this important business, and already a number of
firms are awaiting the completion of the road to enable
them to embark largely in it."

There are 500 miles additional of as good pine forest for
the manufacture of naval stores on the line of this road as
are the ninety miles of which Capt. Smith speaks in his report.

CATTLE.

The Peninsula of Florida is four hundred miles in length, from north to south, having an average breadth of ninety miles. No railroad has yet penetrated this vast region south of the Florida Railroad. Excepting such portions of it as are under cultivation, it is devoted exclusively to the raising of cattle, which pasture winter and summer upon the grasses growing everywhere equally well at all seasons of the year, in forest and on prairie alike. Millions of cattle roam over this country, and stock-growers number their herds by tens of thousands. These cattle have been increasing and accumulating until now the country is fully stocked, and many fear already stocked beyond its capacity to support them. The only available market has been that of Havana, whither they were carried by steamers and sailing vessels from Charlotte's Harbor. Otherwise they were driven several hundred miles, either to Savannah or Augusta. The market has not been equal to the increase, and the opening of this railway will open the markets of the North for these cattle, and greatly facilitate their transportation to Cuba.

FRUITS FROM ABROAD.

From the New York Tribune of August 4, 1877:

Fruit from Abroad.—The extent of the foreign fruit importation to this city is far greater than is generally known. Until recently the business was carried on almost entirely by sailing vessels, but the establishment of steamship lines from the various Mediterranean ports to this city has largely increased its volume. The boats of the Mediterranean and New York Steamship Line, which has now been in operation for about three years, and of a line started this year by Italian dealers, are almost entirely given up to this class of freight.

Steamers arrive every week or ten days during the fruit
season. They make the trip in from twenty to twenty-two
days, and the fruit, which is generally in excellent condition,
is in great demand. The voyage under sail averages about
sixty days.

About 40 per cent. of the fruit brought from Mediterranean
ports now come in steamships. Even with this advantage
the trade is a risky one, but not so much so as with sailing
vessels, liable at any time to long voyages and consequent
destruction of cargoes. The shipments of green fruit begin
early in the Summer with lemons from Malaga, which last
until November, and then continue with the same fruit from
Sicily, which comes through the Winter and until June.
During the last three years there have been large shipments
of oranges from the Adriatic, which arriving here in good
condition, find a ready sale. The shipment of dried fruits is
almost wholly confined to the steamship lines, and includes
large quantities of raisins from Malaga and Valencia, and
currants from Greece. The annual importations reach about
1,000,000 boxes from Malaga, and about 350,000 boxes from
Valencia, and of the total amount about 85 per cent. is consigned to New York firms. The importation of currants is
increasing from year to year, the lower duties stimulating
consumption. The importation now reaches nearly 10,000
tons a year, and nearly all comes to this city. The dried
fruit traffic alone amounts to about $4,000,000 a year. Of
green fruits arriving by steamship there is an average each
year of 100,000 boxes of oranges from Sicily and 75,000 boxes
from Spain, together with 50,000 boxes of lemos from Spain,
500,000 boxes from Sicily, and during the Summer from
15,000 to 40,000 boxes from France, according to the crop.
The consumption in this city reaches nearly 1,000 boxes

daily, the rest going to various parts of the country. The
prices vary from $1.50 to $6.50 a box for oranges and from
$2.50 to $12.50 a box for lemons, according to the season and
the supply.

TROPICAL AND SEMI-TROPICAL FRUITS.

The following is valuable as showing, first—the large quantities of fruit imported to the United States; second—the
heavy loss sustained by the importers by reason of the long
sea voyage; third—the very large savings that would accrue
to the importers if the times in which fruits is in transit was
reduced to three or four days, instead of 6, 8 or 10 days, and
often out so long that a whole cargo is lost at sea; and fourth
—indirectly showing how great would become the production
of these fruits on the Florida Peninsula.

If the West India Islands, Central and South American
fruits could be tranported from the orchards to the northern
markets by fast steamers to Key West, and thence in refrigerating cars, thereby insuring to the producer a sure market
and the importers against loss by delay, by reason of long sea
voyages in a tropical and semi-tropical climate, all the fruits
mentioned in this article, and many others which are too liable
to decay ever to be seen in the northern markets of the United
States, but which, by refrigerating compartments on the
steamers and refrigerating cars, can be taken to every city of
the United States as fresh as when they were gathered from
the trees— as easily, indeed, as fruits are now brought from
California to the markets of the east and south in the same
manner.

The production of these fruits in Florida will mark a development never yet hoped for, and the importations will keep
full pace with their production until tropical fruits will become

as common and cheap in the northern markets as the apple of the Northern States.

A REVIEW OF THE TRADE—VARIETIES IMPORTED, AND THE AMOUNT. OFFICIAL STATISTICS.

Below we give a carefully considered synopsis of the foreign fruit trade of New York for a single year, especially prepared by Inspector Bostwick, of the Customs Department :

Box Fruit.—" The importation of the box fruit at the port of New York, from the Mediteranean ports, during each month of the year was as follows, viz. : In January, 65,456 boxes of oranges and 22,441 boxes of lemons ; in February, 19,525 boxes of oranges and 5,482 boxes of lemons; in March, 73,838 boxes of oranges and 24,55 boxes of lemons ; in April 190,051 boxes of oranges and 97,851 boxes of lemons; in May, 73,590 boxes of oranges and 52,644 boxes of lemons : in June, 18,355 boxes of oranges and 28,399 boxes of lemons ; in July, 5,150 boxes of oranges and 32,308 boxes of lemons : in August, 181 boxes of oranges and 23,302 boxes of lemons ; in September, 8,946 lemons ; in October, 2,667 boxes of lemons ; in November, 827 boxes of oranges and 11,698 boxes of lemons ; in December, 27,846 boxes of oranges and 6,226 boxes of lemons. The above comprise 792,372 boxes, of which 474,849 were oranges and 317,523 were lemons. There were 31 cargoes by steamers and 124 by sailing vessels—which shows an increase of 6 cargoes by steamers and 20 cargoes by sailing vessels over the number of importations the previous year, while the number of boxes of fruit in excess of the importations of the same year was only 5,675. There was also imported from Palermo about 4,000 boxes of mandarines, a variety of small orange, containing from forty to fifty in a box. The percentage of loss was twenty-five per cent. The total number of oranges was 112,462,600, and of lemons 114,408,280. The average percentage of loss˙on box fruit by decay far exceeds that of the previous, and in fact, was greater than at any˙ period within the last twenty-five years. As a necessary consequence, the losses of importers, in the aggregate was correspondingly large. This heavy loss was mostly confined to that of oranges, more especially on the importations from Palermo during the months of March, April and May, which comprised about one-half of the whole number of boxes imported during the year. The amount of loss is mainly attributable to the length of time consumed in making the voyage which was from 80 to 120 days. It is to be regretted that no better success has attended the efforts of the importers of Mediterranean fruit for the past few years. When we take into consideration the large amount of capital involved in this hazardous branch of commerce, and the not unfrequent and heavy losses sustained by them, we cannot but wonder at and admire their perseverance and courage, which certainly merits a much richer reward than has recently fallen to their lot.

West India Fruit.—"The trade in West India fruit has proved anything but satisfactory or profitable to the importors and others who were engaged in it during the year, and it may with propriety be here stated, that the above remarks in relation to the Mediterranean fruit trade, and to those who were engaged in it, will apply with equal force to the importers of West India fruit, whose losses during the past two years have also been very large.

Oranges from the West Indies.—"The importation of oranges from the West Indies during the year consisted of forty-five cargoes, by sailing vessels, from Mayaguez and Ponce, Porto Rico ; Kingston, Jamaica ; Havana and Baracoa, Cuba ; Matanzas, Martinique, Abaco, Harbor Island,

San Domingo and Hayti, comprising 17,816,735 oranges. This includes 19,046 barrels, nearly all of which were imported in steamers from Havana, Kingston and Nassau—a decrease of fifteen cargoes and 4,601,496 oranges under the importations of the previous year. The number of oranges that perished in the voyage, 9,900,259—equivalent to a loss of fifty·five per cent. The decrease in the number of importations of oranges was in nowise owing to the lack of fruit in the West Indies. On the contrary, the orange crop was a bountiful one, but was solely on account of the losses on the importations already made. The number of barrels of oranges per steamers, in excess of the importations of last year, was 9,478.

Bananas.—" The importation of bananas during the year exceeded that of any former year. There were 150 cargoes, of which 143 were from Baracoa ; 4 from Kingston, Jamaica ; 2 from Utilla, and one from Ruatan, Central America ; showing an increase of forty-eight cargoes in excess of the importations of 1871. The total number of bunches of bananas imported was 401,670, of which 344,280 were from Baracoa, an increase of 100,000 in excess of the importations of last year from the latter place ; 5,686 were from Jamaica, and, 3,750 from Utilla and Rautan. The loss by decay was twenty-nine per cent. There were also imported from Aspinwall, in steamers, 53,640 bunches bananas—an increase of 10,223 bunches in excess of the importations of the previous year from the same place. The loss on these importations was equal to thirty-three per cent. The trade in Aspinwall bananas has materially increased within the past few years. Formerly only a few hundred bunches were occasionally imported in steamers plying between Aspinwall and this city, where now, and for several years past, thousands of bunches are monthly imported.

Pineapples.—" The importations of pineapples from Eleuthera, Matanzas, Havana, Nassau, Abaco and Harbor Island, consisted of ninety cargoes, and comprised 4,190,051 pineapples, showing a small increase over the number imported last year. The number that perished on the voyage was 983,-826, being a loss of twenty-four per cent.

Cocoanuts.—" The importation of cocoanuts at this port during the year consisted of 174 cargoes, of which 143 were from Baracoa, and the residue from San Blas, San Andreas, San Antonio, San Domingo, Carthagena, Ruatan, Old Providence and Kingston, Jamaica, and comprised 7,990,041 cocoanuts (including those imported from Aspinwall in steamers), of which number 1,036,355, perished on the voyage—showing a loss of thirteen per cent., and an increase of 970,108 cocoanuts in excess of the importations of last year.

Miscellaneous.—" The importation of limes from the West Indies and Aspinwall during the year comprised 537 barrels, on which there was a loss by decay of thirty-six per cent. The number of shaddocks imported last year was only 21,-128, on which there was a loss of forty per cent. The shaddock is not a desirable fruit for eating, it is mostly used for making marmalade. The quantity of grape fruits imported was small. The whole number comprised only 13,700, and the loss was thirty-six per cent. The above shows a small decrease under the importation of last year. Of plantains 36,550 were imported during the year, and the loss by decay was thirty per cent. The quantity of pomegranates, mangoes, sapodillas and many—apples something less than the importation of last year. Nearly the whole of them perished in the voyage.

Cantaloupe Melons.—Less than 500 cantaloupe melons were imported from Malaga during the year, thirty per cent. of which perished on the voyage.

Disasters at Sea.—This year will long be remembered by many with sorrow and regret as one noted for the great number of disasters which occurred at sea, and which resulted not only in the total destruction of scores of vessels, but also in the loss of hundreds of the lives of hardy seamen. It would seem to be superfluous to say that the perils of the sea were unusually great and almost innumerable, as the fact must be patent to every one who has noticed the passing events of the year. The vessels engaged in the West India fruit trade the past year were, unfortunately, not an exception to the prevailing fatality.

Cultivation of Semi-Tropical Fruit in the South.—The increased attention paid to the cultivation of many varieties of semi-tropical fruit in certain sections of our own country, within the past few years, has proved not only quite satisfactory but also remunerative to those who have embarked in the enterprise. Comparatively speaking, but few persons are aware of the existence or extent of the numerous orange groves in the States of Florida and Louisiana, more especially in the first named State. Some of them were planted many years since, and others more recently and within the last thirty years. The products of these orange groves for several years past have been abundant, yielding many millions of oranges of an excellent quality. A ready market and remunerative prices were found for the surplus fruit over and above the requirements for home consumption, principally in Savannah and Charleston, only a small portion of it finding its way to the Northern States.

Lemons, of large size and superior quality, are now successfully raised in East Florida, but not in quantities sufficient for export. Other varieties of fruit are also cultivated, such as limes, grape fruit, pomegranates, guava apples, olives, figs, the date palm, Japan plum and pineapples.

The Trade in Green Fruit.—"From the official records of the Custom House the following tables have been condensed. They exhibit the values of all the green fruit imported from the Mediterranean, the West Indies and Central and South America, as well as the amount of duty collected, and they are, therefore, calculated to give at a glance a correct idea of the extent of the trade of this port in green fruit.

	Value.	Duty.
Oranges and lemons (20 per cent. duty)	$2,085,879	$417,175 80
Pineapples (20) per cent. duty	159,631	31,926 20
Bananas and other green fruit (10 per cent duty	500,426	50,014 40
Cocoanuts	158,509	9,993 20
Total	$2,904,445	$509,138 60

"A comparison of the two sets of figures given above shows an increase of the amount in value of green fruit imported $314,419, and of duty $29,070,40, over the amount in value and duty of the imports of green fruit last year. So much for the facts connected with the importation of green fruit at the port of New York. To follow it thence to its destination in various parts of the country would be very interesting, but would exceed the limits the writer has set for himself in the preparation of these yearly statements. It can readily be imagined that the same degree of risk which attends its im-, portation follows the later dealing in this most perishable commodity, although it is undoubtedly true that the risk assumed by the importers is the greatest experienced in the trade, both from the greater amount of their ventures and from the fact that they are subjected to the delays and dangers peculiar to sea traffic."

A thousand oranges may be purchased in Havana for about $4.75, and their value here may be about $20 a thousand, but the fruit must be sound when it is sold, so that the profits on it are by no means so large as might at first be supposed. The annual loss on imported grape fruit and shaddocks is frequently as much as twenty per cent.; limes, fifteen per cent.; and on mangoes it is impossible almost to estimate it. It is a fruit extremely difficult of preservation, and very often a whole cargo is destroyed on the voyage from the West Indies.

Pineapples and Cocoanuts.—There is probably as great a demand for pineapples in New York as for any species of imported fruit. Their very perishable nature is best shown by the enormous profits which importers expect to realize on the sound fruit. They cost between $33 and $34 a thousand in West Indies, and are sold here for about $120 a thousand. The average loss on pineapples by decay on shipboard is about thirty per cent., and on bananas about twenty-five per cent.; on grape fruit thirty per cent., and on cocoanuts probably not more than fifteen per cent.

An immense number of cocoanuts are brought to New York every year. Those from the South America are esteemed very much finer than those coming from Baracoa, the former frequently selling in this city for $65 a thousand. while the latter seldom brings more than $38. Their average cost at the ports of shipment is about $20 a thousand, and the profits of the business are very large.

FROM SCRIBNER'S MAGAZINE.

Fruit Culture in Florida.—But very little capital is needed for the starting of a grove, and the rewards of a successful one are very great. Oranges sell at from $25 to $68 per thousand in Jacksonville, and are readily transportable to any of the Atlantic seaports. When the necessary dredging and building of canals has been accomplished, so that the Indian river may have an outlet via the St. Johns, the North will be supplied with oranges of more delicate texture than any it has yet seen; and the number of groves along the river will be legion. The fitness of Florida for the growth of the tropical and semi-tropical fruits is astonishing. Not only do the orange, the lemon, the lime, and the citron flourish there, but the peach, the grape, the fig, the pomegranate, the plum, all varieties of berries, the olive, the banana, and the pineapple grow luxuriantly. Black Hamburg and White Muscat grapes fruit finely in the open air; the Concord and Scuppernong are grown in vast quantities. The guava, the tamarind, the wonderful alligator pear, the plantain, the cocoanut and the date, the almond and the pecan, luxuriate in Southern Florida. We have within our boundaries a tropic land, rich and strange, which will in future years be inhabited all winter long by thousands of families, and where beautiful towns and perhaps cities will spring up.

DISTANCE OF SEVERAL DOMESTIC AND FOREIGN PORTS FROM KEY WEST.

U. S. Coast Survey Office, }
Washington, August 23d, 1877. }

Dear Sir :

By request I send you a table of distances asked for. * *

By direction of the Superintendent.

J. E. HILGARD,

Assistant Coast Survey in charge of Office.

Distance from Key West to the various ports of the United States, Cuba and other countries in nautical miles :

MILES.

Key West to Bahia............................... 3910
 "   "   Pernambuco 3535
 "   "   Rio Grande do Sul.................... 5322
 "   "   Rio Janeiro.......................... 4600
 ..   "   Buenos Ayres 5720
 "   "   Montevideo 5610
From Panama to Callao 1772
 "   "   to Cobija........................... 2132
 "   "   to Valparaiso....................... 2640
Sand Key Light at Key West to Mora Light Havana.. 82.3

GEORGIA,

The general character of the eastern portion of this State
is a sandy loam, the basis of the soil being clay. The soil
is fertile, much of it exceedingly so. The principal part of
the timber is the yellow pine of the Southern States, and of
great value for lumber. A fuller account is given of it on
another page.

Along the rivers and smaller streams are large quantities
of live oak and other timber of many varieties and very great
value.

The timber will for a half century afford an endless supply
of lumber and a source of great wealth.

The land on the entire line of the road, with trifling exceptions, is susceptible of high and profitable cultivation. In
natural resources this country ranks with the best agricultural regions of the Southern States.

The return of the value of taxable property in this State
for the year 1870, being the last made, is :

Aggregate value of land.................... $95,600,674
City and town property.....................   47,922,514
National Bank shares,..............   985,900

Money and solvent debts................... 26,646,995

Merchandise......,... 12,834,118

Shipping................................ 214,775

Stocks and bonds........................ 5,482,765

Cotton manufactories......... 2,985,498

Iron works, etc......... 658,026

Mining... 33,140

Value of household and kitchen furniture..... 1,519,857

Plantation and mechanical tools............ 162,859

Value of all other property................. 30,933,568

Making a total value of all property of... $226,119,528

EASTERN GEORGIA.

That portion of Georgia between Millen and the Saint Mary's River, and immediately contiguous to the road, em- braces 16 counties, and contains 131,871 inhabitants.

The following statistics are from the Census Report of 1870:

Farms, acres improved....................... 617,533

" " unimproved.. 3,236,316

Cash value of farms $8,716,730

Estimated value farm products................ 7,944,515

Cash value live stock..................... 3,408,993

Bushels corn.................................. 1,331,988

" oats................................. 239,837

Bales cotton............................. 30,610

Pounds wool.................................. 140,156

Bushels sweet potatoes....................... 475,882

Pounds rice.................................21,734,008

" butter......... 146,488

Gallons Molasses.............................. 121,644

Pounds honey...................... 55,311
Forest products............................. 801,559

FLORIDA PENINSULA.

That portion of Florida, on the Peninsula, lying immedi- ately on and contiguous to this road embraces 18 counties, and contains 82,015 inhabitants, as shown by the last census. These counties are rapidly filling up. The following statistics are also from the census last taken :

Farms, acres improved...................... 284,049
    "   " unimproved................... 800,488
Cash value farms......................... $4,175,592
Estimated value farm products.............. 3,714,316
Cash value live stock................ 2,963,656
Bushels corn............................. 770,105
Bushels oats............................. 24,453
Bales cotton............................. 10,905
Pounds wool............................. 15,308
Bushels sweet potatoes.................... 489,124
Pounds rice............................. 151,088
Gallons molasses......................... 103,496
Hogsheads sugar............. 593
Pounds honey............................. 5,247
Estimated value real and personal estate...... $18,706,786

(*Total area of Georgia and Florida.*)

Georgia, square miles........ ..·········.......... 58,000
Florida, " 59,248

Total square miles...................... 117,248

6

4

UNITED STATES LANDS IN FLORIDA.

From the Annual Report of the Commissioner General Land Office for the year ending June 30, 1876.

Tabular Statement showing the number of Acres of public Lands surveyed, in the following land States and Territories up to June 30, 1875, including the present year and the total of the public Lands surveyed up to June 30, 1876, also the total area of the public domain remaining unsurveyed with in the same.

FLORIDA.

Area of public Lands in the State:

Acres,...... :........................... 37,406,520

Square Miles, ... 59,268

Total surveys up to June 30, 1876 :

Acres,...... 30,028,152

Public Lands unsurveyed up to June 30, 1876, inclusive of private land claims :

Acres........................ 7,903,368

Statement exhibiting the quantity of land patented to the several States under the Acts of Congress approved September 28, 1850, and March 12, 1860.

FLORIDA.

Acres,............................... 10,735,403

FLORIDA.

The large amount of United States lands in the State of Florida, and especially in the peninsula of Florida, which it would be most advantageous to the Government to open to settlement and cultivation, induces us to insert the following description of the State, its soil and resources.

DESCRIPTION OF THE COUNTRY AND ITS PRODUCTIONS.

The following account of Florida and its productions is from an official document published by the State :

Geography.—The geography of Florida is unique, and is of special interest, because many of the important characteristics of the State, which seems to be contradictory, if not impossible, are easily explained by a consideration of its peculiar position and geographical character.

The shape of Florida is somewhat like that of a boot upside down, the foot part extending northwardly, and the leg pointing to the south. The foot part thus extends 350 miles, from east to west, while the leg, or the peninsula proper, extends southwardly over 400 miles.

The State contains 59,268 square miles, or 37,931,520 acres.

The whole territory lies within the region denominated as "hot" by the Physical Geographers. But the results that might be expected from its geographical location are materially affected by its peninsula shape, and its oceanic surroundings.

The peninsula averages in width about ninety miles, and is fanned by the Gulf winds on one side and the Trade winds on the other ; and thus, every portion is exposed to the balmy and vivifying influences of almost constant oceanic winds, and from all these geographical peculiarities have resulted a pleasantness and salubrity of climate, and a power of vegetable production, so wonderful as to be almost incredible.

The surface of the State is, as a whole, remarkably level, though this is more characteristic of the eastern and western portion than of the central part.

Perhaps the most marked of the geographical features of the State is to be found in the enormous extent of her coast line, which on the Atlantic and the Gulf exceeds 1,100 miles. The coast line is also remarkable for the great number of large bays and estuaries, which furnish facilities for commercial intercourse that will hasten the development of the resources of Florida beyond the expectations of the most sanguine.

Another marked geographical feature of the State is found in the number of large and navigable streams. The Appalachicola, the Suwanee, the St. Mary's and the St. John's would be noticeable rivers anywhere. The St. John's is one of the most surprising rivers on the globe. When it is considered that there is not an eminence in East Florida which attains the height of 200 feet, and that the St. John's winds through a level region, strangers are struck with astonishment as they ascend the river and find its average breadth two miles or more for 200 miles from its mouth. The ebb and flow of the tide are quite perceptible at the upper end of Lake George, more than 150 miles from the ocean.

Although the general character of the soil of Florida is sandy, still few portions of the whole United States are more bountifully provided with water, and that easily accessible. Springs of all kinds, some of clear sweet water, some strongly impregnated with sulphur, and others characterized by various mineral admixtures, are so abundant as to be little noticed. Some of these springs are of gigantic proportions, so large that complete rivers rush at once from the very bowels of the earth.

History.—The following is a brief abstract of the leading facts in the history of Florida. What a picture it presents! Discovered in 1496, permanently settled in 1565, ceded to Great Britain in 1763, with a population of only six hundred, after a colonial existence of two hundred years, receded to Spain in 1784, sold and ceded to the United States in 1819, receiving a territorial government in 1822, admitted to the Union in 1845, seceding in 1861, and reconstructed in 1868; sacked and pillaged repeatedly by Europeans; shifting its nationality from time to time, and losing almost its entire population by each change; harassed and plundered by repeated Indian wars from 1816 to 1858, and just as prosperity began to dawn, plunged into a four years' war, she has suffered every evil, political and social, that does not involve absolute extinction.

The wonder truly is, not that she has not attained a more flourishing condition, but that she exists at all, and that her boundless forests, her lovely rivers, and her beautiful lakes are not fast locked in the silent embrace of a moveless desolation.

Without such reference to her previous history there would be an irreconcilable discrepancy between the present condition of Florida and that which might naturally be expected from a consideration of her fertility, her climate and her resources.

Soil.—The extreme eastern and western parts of the State have a soil more or less underlaid with clay or marl, and interspersed to a greater or less extent with what are called " hammocks," or lands covered with a growth of hard wood.

But as one proceeds westward along the northern boundary of the State, the character of the soil changes from sand to loam, and then to a strong clay soil, until, in Leon, Gadsden, Jackson, and other counties, a large part of the soil is composed of a strong and rather heavy clay. Then taking a stretch of land in the northern tier of counties, ex-

tending from Madison to Jackson, inclusive, and thence down
the Gulf, and extending along the Gulf coast from Liberty
to Hernando, and including Sumpter, Marion, Alachua, Levy
and other counties, one can find almost every conceivable
variety of soil, adapted to the growth of nearly every crop
that can be selected. Here, really, in the counties above
mentioned, with whose characters strangers are almost entirely unacquainted, is the very cream and flower of the State
of Florida.

That which is denominated " first rate pine land" in Florida has nothing analogous to it in any of the other States.
Its surface is covered for several inches deep with a dark vegetable mould, beneath which, to the depth of several feet, is
a chocolate-colored sandy loam, mixed, for the most part, with
limestone pebbles, and resting on a substratum of marl, clay,
or limestone rock. The fertility and durability, of this description of land may be estimated from the well-known fact
that it has, on the Upper Suwanee, and in several other districts, yielded during twenty years of successive cultivation,
without the aid of manure, four hundred pounds of Sea Island cotton to the acre. These lands are still as productive
as ever, so that the limit of their durability is yet unknown.

The " second rate pine" lands, of Florida, are all productive. These lands affords fine natural pasturage; they are
heavily timbered with the best species of pitch and yellow
pine; they are, for the most part, high, rolling, healthy, and
well watered. They are generally based upon marl, clay, or
limestone. They will produce for many years without the
aid of manure, and when manured they will yield two thousand pounds of the best quality of sugar to the acre, or
about three hundred pounds of Sea Island Cotton. They

will, besides, when properly cultivated, produce the finest Cuba tobacco, oranges, lemons, limes, and various other tropical productions, which must in many instances render them more valuable than the best bottom lands in the more northern States.

Even the lands of the "third rate," or most inferior class, are by no means worthless under the climate of Florida. This class of lands may be divided into two orders; the one comprising high rolling sandy districts, which are sparsely covered with a growth of "black jack" and pine; the other embracing low, flat, swampy regions, which are frequently studded with "bay galls," and are occasionally inundated, but which are covered with luxuriant vegetation, and, very generally, with valuable timber. The former of these, it is now ascertained, owing to their calcareous soil, are well adapted to the growth of Sisal hemp, which is a valuable tropical production. This plant (the Agave Sisiliana), and the Agave Mexicana hemp, also known as the Maguay, the pulke plant, the century plant, &c., have both been introduced into Florida, and they both grow in great perfection on the poorest lands of the country. As these plants derive their chief support from the atmosphere, they will, like the common air plant, preserve their vitality for many months when left out of the ground.

It is scarcely necessary to add that the second order of the third rate pine lands, as here described, is far from worthless. These lands afford a most excellent range for cattle, besides being valuable for their timber and the naval stores which they will produce.

There is one general feature in the topography of Florida which no other country in the United States possesses, and which affords a great security to the health of its inhabitants. It is this, that the pine lands which form the basis of the country, and which are almost universally healthy, are nearly everywhere studded at intervals of a few miles with hammock lands of the richest quality. These hammocks are not, as is generally supposed, low wet lands; they never require ditching or draining; they vary in extent from a few acres to forty thousand acres, and will probably average about 500 acres each. Hence the inhabitants have it everywhere in their power to select residences either in the pine lands or upon the hammocks as they may desire.

The topographical feature here noted, namely, a general interspersion of rich hammocks, surrounded by high, dry, rolling, healthy pine woods, is an advantage which no other State in the Union enjoys, and Florida forms in this respect a striking contrast with Louisiana, Mississippi and Texas, whose sugar and cotton lands are generally surrounded by vast alluvial regions, subject to frequent inundations, so that it is impossible to obtain, within many miles of them, a healthy residence.

The lands which in Florida are, *par excellence*, denominated "rich lands," are first, the "swamp lands;" second, the "low hammock lands;" third, the "high hammocks;" and fourth, the "first rate pine, oak and hickory lands."

The swamp lands are unquestionably the most durably rich lands in the country. They are the most recently formed lands, and are still annually receiving additions to their surface. They are intrinsically the most valuable lands in Florida, being as fertile as the hammocks and more durable. They are evidently alluvial and of recent formation. They occupy natural depressions or basins, which have been gradually filled up by deposits of vegetable *debris*, etc., washed in from the adjacent and higher lands. Ditching is indispensable to all of them in their preparation for successful cultivation. Properly prepared, however, their inexhaustible fertility sustains a succession of the most sustaining crops with astonishing vigor. The greatest yield of sugar ever realized in Florida was produced on this description of land, viz. : four hogsheads per acre. Sugar cane is here instanced as a measure of the fertility of the soil, because it is one of the most exhausting crops known, and is generally grown without rest or rotation. It is not, however, a fair criterion by which to judge of the relative fertility of lands situated in different climates, for we find on the richest lands in Louisiana the crop of sugar per acre is not more than one hogshead, or about half that of East Florida.

This great disparity in the product of those countries is accounted for, not by any inferiority in the lands of Louisiana or Texas, but by the fact that the early incursions of frost in both these States render it necessary to cut the cane in October, which is long before it has reached maturity; while in East Florida it is permitted to stand, without fear of frost, till December, or till such time as it is fully matured. It is well known that it "tassels" in East Florida, which it never does in either Louisiana or Texas. When cane "tassels" it is evidence of it having reached full maturity.

Low hammocks, which, from the fact of their partaking of the nature of hammocks and swamps, are not inferior to swamp lands in fertility, but perhaps are not quite as durable. They are nearly always level, or nearly so, and have a soil of greater tenacity than that of the high hammocks. The soil in them is always deep. These lands are also extremely well adapted to the growth of the cane, as has been well attested by the many plantations which were formerly in operation here on this description of land.

' *High Hammocks* are the lands in the greatest repute in Florida. These differ from low hammocks in occupying higher ground, and in generally presenting an undulating surface. They are formed of a fine vegetable mould, mixed with a sandy loam in many places several feet deep, and resting in most cases on a substratum of clay, marl or lime- . stone. It will be readily understood by any one at all acquainted with agriculture, that such a soil, in such a climate as Florida, must be extremely productive. This soil scarcely ever suffers from too much wet; nor does drought affect it in the same degree as other lands. High hammock lands produce, with but little labor or cultivation, all the crops of the country in an eminent degree. Such lands have no tendency to break up in heavy masses, nor are they infested with pernicious weeds or grasses. Their extraordinary fertility and productiveness may be estimated by the fact that, in several well known instances in Marion County, three hogsheads of sugar have been made per acre on this description of land, after it had been in cultivation six years, in successive crops of corn, without the aid of fertilizers.

To sum up its advantages, it requires no other preparation than clearing and plowing to fit it at once for the greatest possible production of any kind of crop adapted to the climate. In unfavorable seasons it is much more certain to produce a good crop than any other kind of land, from the fact that it is less affected by exclusively dry or wet weather. It can be cultivated with much less labor than any other lands, being remarkably mellow, and its vicinity is generally high.

The first-rate pine, oak and hickory lands are found in

extensive bodies in many parts of the State, particularly in Marion, Alachua and Hernando counties. From the fact that those lands can be cleared at much less expense than the swamp and hammock lands, they have heretofore been preferred by small planters, and have proved remarkably productive.

There are, besides the lands already noticed, extensive tracts of savanna lands, which approximate in character, texture of the soil, and period and mode of formation, to the swamp lands, differing only in being destitute of timber.

Probably the largest bodies of rich hammock land in East Florida are to be found in Levy, Alachua, Marion, Hernando and Sumpter counties. There are in Levy county alone not less than one hundred thousand acres of the very best description of sugar lands; and there is but a small proportion in any of the five counties here cited that will not pro-. duce remunerative crops of Sea Island and short staple cotton, without the aid of fertalizers.

Field Crops.—In no State of the Union can so extensive a variety of valuable productions be successfully cultivated as in Florida. Most of the crops grown in the temperate zone flourish in the northern portion of the State. Nearly all the peninsula is adapted to the cultivation of semi-tropical fruits. · At least one half of the entire area of the State is south of the line of frost, and will grow successfully the tropical productions of the West Indies.

Indian Corn.—This is to the mass of the people the "staff of life." It is grown in all parts of the State. On rich bottom lands from fifty to sixty bushels per acre is not uncommon.

Cotton.—In a single year Florida produced 63,322 bales

of ginned cotton. Both the long staple or Sea-Island, and the short staple or upland cotton, are cultivated. There is but little long cotton grown west of the Suwanee river, except in the county of Gadsden, and scarcely any short cotton east of the Suwanee. Two hundred to three hundred pounds of short cotton per acre is a fair yield upon ordinary soils, but five hundred pounds per acre is not an unusual crop on strong land. Long cotton produces from one hundred to two hundred pounds per acre as an average crop, but under favorable circumstances three hundred and even four hundred pounds have been raised.

Sugar Cane can be raised on almost any of the soils of the State, on some, of course, more successfully than others; in far the greater portion of the State it rattoons, or springs up from the old roots, and so does not for several years require re-planting: it produces more largely and is more easily cultivated in Florida than in any other State, not excepting Louisiana.

It is a circumstance of frequent and common occurrence for $300 and over to be realized from the produce of sugar and molasses made from the cane grown on one acre only of our common pine lands.

Instances of 19, 21, and of 24 barrels of syrup made to the acre in Gadsden county, are reported.

Statistical returns from Marion, Alachua, Suwanee, and Orange counties, make 2,500 lbs. of sugar per acre, an average return for good cultivation. Accounts from Hernando county give 2,600, 3,400, and 3,600 lbs. of sugar as the actual product per acre of three sugar crops in 1869, in that county, thus giving an average of 3,200 lbs. to the acre.

It is computed that one gallon of syrup will make five

pounds of sugar. Twenty forty-gallon barrels of syrup, therefore, would give four thousand pounds of sugar, and four hogsheads of sugar have been made to the acre in this State.

In Middle and South Florida it grows to ten and twelve feet in height, and in South Florida has grown to the height of seventeen feet. There it matures, tassels and produces seed.

There are millions of acres in Florida that can and will produce easily two thousand pounds of sugar to the acre ; and many of our most intelligent planters firmly believe that the pine lands fertilized will produce a better quality of sugar than can be raised on the black, so called " sugar lands."

Sweet Potatoes.—Next to Indian corn, the most important article of vegetable food in common use is the sweet potato. They do best on light soil. The yield per acre is from 100 to 300 bushels depending upon the season, culture, and quality of soil. They are propagated from the seed, like Irish potatoes ; from draws, and from the vines. The crop is a profitable one and deserving of more attention, as a market crop, than it has hitherto received. Sweet potatoes bear shipment well, and always command good prices in the Northern markets.

Irish Potatoes.—This crop does not produce as well as at the North, but is off in time to be followed by a crop of sweet potatoes the same year. They should be planted in December and January, although good crops are sometimes obtained from later planting. The potatoes are fit for digging in April and May. They can be shipped without difficulty, and at a moderate expense, to the Northern markets, where early potatoes always bring a good price.

Rice.—There is much land in Florida well adapted to the culture of rice. It has been raised to quite an extent. Forty to sixty bushels per acre of rough rice is an average crop, and may be cultivated to advantage in many locations. It is much used as an article of food by all classes.

Tobacco.—Cuba tobacco was largely cultivated in the County of Gadsden before the war, and to some extent in some other portions of the State. Three cuttings in a season are produced from the same stalks. Tobacco is an exhaustive crop, and requires a fertile soil, and its cultivation may be made extremely profitable. Seven hundred pounds to the acre is an average yield.

Indigo.—Under the British occupation of Florida, indigo was the principal staple. It is a sure crop. The plant has become naturalized or is indigenous, and is found growing wild in various parts of the State, and may be cultivated extensively.

Sisal Hemp.—Dr. Henry Perine introduced the Sisal Hemp into South Florida twenty-five years ago, from Yucatan. It is a tropical plant. The soil and climate of south Florida is well adapted to its growth. It is no longer an experiment, as to the growth of the plant, the amount of the product or the value of the fibre. It requires no replanting and very little care after the first year or two. A ton of cleaned hemp can be made to the acre.

Castor Bean.—The Palma Christi, or castor bean, grows luxuriantly. In the southern portion of the State it is perennial, and attains the size of a small tree.

Silk.—At one time silk-growing received considerable attention at St. Augustine. The conditions for a successful prosecution of the business seem peculiarly favorable. The mulberry is a native of our forests Cocoons of the silk-worm are often found. The climate is more mild than that of Italy, and there is no reason why the mulberry tree should not be cultivated, and the silk worm raised with profit.

Coffee.—We know no reason why coffee should not be grown successfully south of the 28th parallel. More than forty years ago a Philadelphia Company sent out an expedition to explore the country and select suitable spots for the cultivation of the coffee plant; but the project was abandoned, Congress refusing the grant of lands required by the Company. Both our climate and soil are found suitable for the culture of coffee, and it cannot fail to become, in a few years, an important item.

Pea Nuts.—The pea-nut grows well on almost any warm, light soil. A hundred bushels to the acre is an average crop. They produce an oil equal to the finest olive oil.

Ramie.—The Ramie plant has been recently introduced. The plant produces a fibre of fine quality and glossy whiteness, which is used in manufacturing cloths, either by itself or mixed with silk or wool. It is a hardy and vigorous grower, and in this climate, perennial. The fibre of the Ramie is stronger than the best European hemp; it may be spun as fine as flax, and it is doubly durable, it will produce from three to five annual crops, each equal to the best gathered from hemp.

Arrow-root.—The Koonta, or Indian arrow-root, grows wild in the southern portion of the peninsula. It was formerly manufactured quite extensively; the sole labor consisting of bringing it from the forest lands and conveying it to the mill; the simple stirring occasioned by the digging being sufficient to secure a better crop than the one just removed.

The Bermuda arrow-root also flourishes, producing, even

on pine lands, from two to three hundred bushels per acre. The yield of merchantable arrow-root flour is from six to eight lbs. to the bushel.

Wheat, Rye, and Oats.—Wheat grows in the northern part of this State. Rye and oats are raised to some extent, chiefly as forage crops.

GARDEN VEGETABLES.

The growing of vegetables for the Northern markets has not, until recently, received much attention. Vegetables grown here can be placed in the markets of the Northern seaboard cities from six weeks to two months earlier than from any other State. As far south as Enterprise, nearly all the vegetables cultivated in a market garden can be ripened any month in the year. Some parties have engaged in the business quite extensively. The chief difficulty is that of transportation. Florida will become, at no distant day, the early market garden for all the Northern cities.

Tomatoes.—The tomato is easily cultivated, and produces abundantly. Early lots sell for almost marvellous prices in New York, and other eastern cities—$1,200 has been netted from a single acre. They will yield from four hundred to five hundred bushels to the acre. South of Palatka they ripen in the field every month in the year.

Cucumbers.—In May last, Florida cucumbers were quoted at $8 to $10 per hundred in the New York market. The plant has to contend with few of the enemies so destructive at the North. It bears shipment exceedingly well.

Melons.—There is no country where the watermelon attains so great perfection as in Florida, and we might add, where they can be raised with less care. The muskmelon and cantaloup also flourish. Great quantities have been shipped the past season, and profitably laid down in New York, and other Northern Cities.

Peas.—Soils that contain some lime, quite rich and moderately moist, are the best for peas. The month of January is the best time to plant. The crop will then be ready for market in April, at which season green peas command high prices all over the country. They bear shipment well, and are a profitable crop, and were transportation quick and easy they would be raised in great abundance. •

Beans.—Beans of all kinds grow well, particularly the Lima bean. The Lima is found in almost every garden. Snap-beans are very prolific, and their culture for shipment like the Pea is worthy of attention.

Cabbages and Turnips.—Cabbages succeed best in winter. Sown in the fall they will produce fine heads in the spring months of April and May. Turnips can be had fresh every month in the year, and are particularly a valuable winter crop. Cauliflower, brocoli, and kohl-rabi are grown without difficulty. The latter is very common in the eastern market.

Beets, &c.—Beets do best in a deep, rich, moist soil. For winter use, plant in September or October; for summer, in January or February. Carrots and parsnips should be treated in the same manner.

Miscellaneous Crops.—All the vegetables usually cultivated in a good family garden can be raised. Squashes are grown with great ease and of the best quality. Onions, lettuce, radishes, celery, etc., etc., grow to perfection ; also peppers, parsley, etc. Asparagus and rhubarb succeed with the usual attention. The egg-plant does finely. Okra is found growing in every garden. It is highly prized.

FRUITS.

There can be but one opinion as to the fitness of Florida

7

for the growth of tropical and semi-tropical fruits. In this respect Florida enjoys a monopoly which will make her one of the richest and most important of the United States. Oranges, lemons, pineapples, and various other tropical fruits, to which it is the adaptability of the climate to these productions that makes even the inferior lands of Florida susceptible of producing crops more valuable than those of the best lands in other parts of the Union.

Oranges.—The orange belongs to the *citrus* family, in which are included the lemon, lime, citron, shaddock and similar fruits. The varieties are numerous. In their native state they continue flowering nearly all the summer, and for a considerable portion of the year. Every stage of growth, the bud, flower, green and ripe fruit, can be seen on the tree at the same time. The sour orange and the bitter-sweet grow wild upon the St. John's and Indian rivers, and in many parts of the peninsula.

The primeval woods on the banks of the Indian river are vast gardens of the sour wild orange. These oranges are to be found in nearly every part of the woods. The orange is a sure crop. The tree is long-lived and has very few enemies.

The oranges of Florida are celebrated for their superior quality. At present the best method of establishing a grove is to set out the wild orange trees, and, at the proper time, bud them with the sweet orange. The sour trees may be dug up at any time during the winter and transplanted. The tree usually commences bearing the third year from transplanting. They are brought from the hammocks on the upper St. John's. The orange will grow upon almost any soil.

A grove in full bearing should average eight hundred to the tree. Many trees will bear from one thousand to three thousand, and some as high as seven thousand per year.

In Jacksonville oranges have sold, the past season at from twenty-five to sixty dollars per thousand. Taking eight hundred as the average per tree, and one hundred trees to the acre, and we have eighty thousand oranges from an acre, which, at thirty dollars per thousand, which may be taken as the average price, will give two thousand four hundred dollars; while at twenty-five dollars, the lowest price at which good oranges were sold, we have two thousand dollars as the income from a single acre. It requires no great outlay of capital to start an orange grove, and its care involves no more labor than the care of an apple orchard of the same size. We leave it for parties interested to calculate the profits, arising from an orange grove of ten acres in full bearing. We are quite sure that the credit side of the sheet will show that the profit of growing the orange is larger in proportion to the expenditure of money and labor than that derived from the cultivation of any other crop grown in the United States.

Lemons, Limes, Citrons, etc.—It will be unnecessary to go into detail regarding these fruits, since the remark we have made in regard to the soil, climate, and culture required for the orange will apply equally to them. The lemon is a trifle more hardy than the orange. The Sicily lemon, budded on the sour or bitter-sweet orange, does finely.

The lime is a prolific bearer, and a most wholesome and excellent fruit. In South Florida the tree is in bearing nearly the whole year. A good business could be done at raising them for the juice, which is an article of commerce.

The citron grows on a straggling bush, which requires support while the fruit is ripening. They are six to eight inches in diameter, of a rich yellow color, hanging from the slender branches, fitting emblems of the golden fruits of autumn The citron does well wherever the orange flourishes.

The shaddock resembles a large lemon.

Peaches.—The peach attains its highest degree of perfection at the South. The trees possess more vigor and greater longevity than at the North. So well adapted is the climate to the growth of the peach, that they are found growing wild by the road-sides and in the corners of the fences. With communication, there will be no difficulty in shipping them to New York, where, during the months of May and June, they would command high prices.

Grapes.—The South is the true home of the grape. It is found wild in the forests of Florida, and grows luxuriantly. In the southern part of the State three crops of grapes in a year are gathered. The Black Hamburg, White Muscat, Golden Chessalas, and other foreign grapes, grow and fruit, finely in the open air. The Concord succeeds well, and is so much improved that it is nearly equal in quality to the Black Hamburg. The scuppernong is cultivated more widely than any other variety. It makes a fine wine.

Figs.—Of all [the fruit cultivated in the South, the fig requires the least care, and is one of the most useful. It is propogated readily from cuttings, which usually bear the second year. During the summer months the fig may be found upon the breakfast tables of all lovers of fine fruit. When ripe, it is mild, rich and luscious. Every one in Florida who owns a foot of land may literally " sit under his own vine and fig tree," as no one thinks of doing without figs.

Pomegranates.—The pomegranate is common in Florida. There are the sweet and sour varieties. The bush is a pretty, ornamental shrub, and, with its beautiful blossoms and pendant fruit, is decidedly ornamental. The rind is very bitter, and has been used as a substitute for Peruvian bark ;

but the juice, which is contained in little sacks surrounding the seeds, is a pleasant acid, and quite agreeable.

Apples, Pears and Quinces.—These fruits are cultivated in the northern part of the State.

Plums, Apricots, and Nectarines.—The plum grows wild all over the State, and some of the varieties are scarcely inferior to many of the cultivated varieties. Apricots and nectarines succeed quite as well as the peach.

Berries.—There is no place where the blackberry is more perfectly at home than in Florida. The huckleberry grows everywhere, and is plentiful in market. The strawberry is easily cultivated, and bears abundant crops. The vines will continue in bearing for six months. The mulberry grows wild, and bears two crops in a year.

The Olive.—The olive has been successfully cultivated. Trees grown from the seed commence bearing the tenth year, and are fully productive about the twentieth or twenty-fifth.

The Banana and Pineapple.—In all the southern portion of the peninsula the banana does finely. The pineapple also succeeds admirably in South Florida. It and the banana are raised from suckers, which come into bearing about eighteen months after being planted. The banana grows to the height of thirty feet; the pineapple to a height of about three feet.

MISCELLANEOUS.

Of strictly tropical fruits that are worthy of attention, in addition to those above noticed, may be mentioned the guava, sappadillo, sugar-apple, tamarind, alligata pear, pawpaw, plantain, cocoa-nut, and the date. All the above are growing luxuriantly in South Florida. The cocoa-nut is a large tree, rising above all the other trees of the forest. The fruit is ripening the year round. The peacan-nut can be raised without difficulty, and the almond.

Stock-Raising.—On much of the land is to be found a large growth of oaks, scattered among the pines, which furnish abundance of mast, on which, in the genial climate of Florida with little care or protection, hogs can be raised *ad libitum*, They are to be found everywhere, throughout the forests of the whole peninsula, half-wild and in good condition, finding easily an independent support.

The whole territory is likewise covered with a more or less thick coat of grasses, which retain their greenness to a greater or less extent throughout the year. Cattle maintain themselves in good condition, entirely without care. In the southern portion of the State are found large prairies, called savannas, covered with tall grasses, which afford good nutriment for cattle. Upon them large herds pasture, which are driven up occasionally by their owners; the beeves selected out, and the calves marked. During the war the Confederates drew large supplies of beef from Florida. Some of the heavy cattle men own as many as twenty-five to thirty thousand head each.

Sheep also do well in Florida, as the climate is warm and suited to their nature.

Timber and Lumber.—Florida is, beyond question, the best timbered State in the Union. On all the least moist and more level portions, the pine is the prevalent forest tree— either the yellow or the pitch-pine. It grows with great beauty, and attains a large size, furnishing some of the handsomest pine lumber to be found in the markets of the world. The extent of the fine lands, and the possible amount of lumber that could be manufactured, would be incredible to one who has never visited the State. There are probably more than 30,000 square miles of heavy pine forest within its limits.

In the moisture lands an almost infinite variety of trees are to be found, of which the more valuable for timber and lumber are live oak, white oak, the hickory, the ash, the birch, the cedar, the magnolia, the sweet bay, and the cypress. Of all these varieties a great abundance is to be found throughout the State. The supply for any purposes of manufacture may well be said to be inexhaustible. The larger proportion of what has loosely been called swamp in Florida is simply low hammock land, with a soil of inexhaustible fertility, and covered with a dense growth of mainly cypress, magnolia and sweet bay.

The timber of the magnolia is susceptible of a variety of uses. It can be brought to a fine polish, and is used for the nicer and finer kinds of wheelwright and cabinet work. Of this timber the supply is very large.

The wood of the red or sweet bay, in fineness of texture and in its other valuable qualities, stands next to mahogany, and is in demand for cabinet work.

The resources of Florida in the direction of the manufacture of wooden ware, and of tools of all descriptions made from wood, have not only never been developed, but have hardly been suspected. If an inexhaustible abundance of material, at the cheapest possible rates, and very great accessibility, are of any value and importance in promoting the success of wooden manufacture, then this bids fair to become a leading industrial pursuit in this State.

Game and Fish.—Everywhere on the coast, both of the ocean and the Gulf, excellent oysters abound. The oysters of St. Andrew's Bay are celebrated throughout the South, and those of Indian River are larger, finer and still more abun-

dant. And off more than half the Florida coast, turtle in
immense quantities and of great size are continually taken.
The capacity of these waters for oysters and turtle is almost
inexhaustible.

Fish, of the best quality, are to be found on all the coasts
and in all the lakes and rivers, forming a cheap, easily attain-
able and very wholesome article of diet, and giving opportunity for business in this direction to almost any extent. It
is no exaggeration to say that the bays and inlets, as well as
rivers, of Florida swarm with valuable fish. Very valuable
shad fisheries may be carried on in various localities.

Turkeys, ducks, squirrels, deer and bear are to be found
throughout the State, and no part of the United States can
furnish a more exciting or agreeable winter hunting ground.

While the North and West are covered with snow, the
hunter in the Indian River region may comfortably camp
out month after month, with a single blanket, taking, as he
needs his sweet potatoes from the ground, and the orange,
lemon and banana from the plantations along the route, and
in the continuous sunshine of an unending spring, surfeit
himself with the pursuit of game.

Sponge.—Key West is the headquarters of the sponge business. Large quantities are annually gathered in the shallow
waters along the coast, and form an immense trade.

AREA AND POPULATION OF THE ITALIAN PEN-
INSULA.

The Italian peninsula contains 58,394 square miles, and
has a population of 11,875,487 people.

A reference to the maps of the Peninsula of Italy and the
Peninsula of Florida, will show the almost exact similarity
in their geographical formation. In climate they are the

same, excepting that the Peninsula of Italy is traversed by a mountain range while Florida is not. This topographical difference makes the central or mountainous region of Italy colder than any portion of the Peninsula of Florida.

— — —

CLIMATE, TOPOGRAPHY AND HEALTFULNESS OF FLORIDA.

The following extracts are taken from an address by Dr. A. S. Baldwin, President of the Medical Association of the State of Florida, before that Association, in the city of Jacksonville, on the 18th day of February, 1875.

Temperature.—To elucidate this we have ample materials, and to make it clear and easily understood I have tabulated the abstracts of mean temperature taken at seventeen stations besides my own. From this we learn that the mean temperature of the spring for the entire state is 71°.62 ; for the summer, 80° 51' ; for autumn, 71° 66' ; for winter, 60° 04' ; and for the year, 70° 95' ; and for the stations on latitude 28° N. ; and south of it, for the spring we have 74° 94' ; for summer 81° 93' for autumn, 76° 57' ; for winter, 63° 59' ; and for the year, 74° 87' ; for the stations north of latitude 28° N, we have for the spring, 70° 66' ; for summer, 80° 10' ; for autumn, 70° 23' ; for winter, 58° 29' ; and for the year, 69° 82'. There is not exhibited any great difference between the northern and southern portions of the state, but enough to afford a choice of temperature during the different seasons if the visitors desire a change. During spring, the temperature south of 28° latitude is 4° 28' higher ; and for summer, 1° 83 ; for autumn, 6° 34' ; and for winter, 5° 40' higher than it is north of of latitude 28°.

The average number of frosts for the month of January, in Jacksonville, (on the northern limit of the state) in twenty-seven years record 5.4; for February,'3.1; for March, 1.3 ; for April, 0.2, and no more until October, 0.2; in November, 2.3; for December, 5.2. The first frosts in the Fall have occurred in October four times ; in November, sixteen times ; in December, seven times; and twice the second frosts has occurred in February. There have been several years in which no frost occurred in October ; there have been years in which none occurred in November or December. There have been years when no frosts occurred in January, none in February, still more in which March was exempt; very few frosts have occurred in April, and none after. In 1858 a frost occurred on the 28th of April, which is the latest recorded ; and there have been but four Aprils in which frosts have been recorded ; and there have been but four Octobers in which they have been recorded. From these statements an idea can be formed of the average amount of freezing in winter. December and January are the oftenest visited with frosts, a little over five times in each month on an average.

As clearness of sky is connected with the subject of radiation, and is also an important element of climate, it will be introduced here. I have, in making up my results, of which I propose to present an abstract, counted those days clear which were marked from 0 up to 5, the latter representing the sky half covered with clouds. The month of January, from twenty-two years' observation, has had an average of 20.3 clear days ; February, for 25 years, 19.5 ; March, for the same period, 20.4 ; April, 25. ; May, for 26 years, 22.1 ; June, for 25 years, 17.1 ; July, for the same period, 18.5 ; August, for 26 years, 19.1 ; September, for 24 years, 17.2 ; October, for 25 years, 19.2 ; November, for 24 years, 20.0 ; December, for the same period, 20.0, clear days. For Spring, the average is 63.7 ; for Summer, 55.1 ; for Autumn, 56.4 ; for Wintor, 59.8; and for tho year, 235 clear days out of 365, leaving 130 days in which the sky was more than half covered with clouds, and on some of which rain has fallen. In January there has been an average of 6.6 rainy days; in February, 3.6; in March, 5.7; and in December 5.4 rainy days, and theso constitute tho four months in which visitors are especially interested. In these months we havo had an average of 21.3 rainy days out of 121 days.

Topography.—In its topography Florida presents no mountains and no elevated plateaus exceeding 300 feet above the sea, by which it is bounded on all sides, except on its northern border. But it is not, as many times represented, a low, flat, marshy country, for in many portions its surface is undulating and rolling. Its area covers 59,248 squaro miles of pine land, oak hammocks, flat savannas, numerous clear, fresh water lakes and rivers, which add beauty to tho landscape, comfort, pleasure, and subsistenco to the inhabitants in their vicinity, for most of the two latter are liberally stocked with fine varieties of fish. Many of our springs and small lakes even are artesian and riso from the substrata of rocks upon which the arable soil is based, and pour out copious streams of water to augment the volume of our rivers, which discharge into the sea. The probable sources of these are in the higher land, on our northern border, and are supplied by the rainfall of neighboring States. The State is, in somo portions, traversed by subterranean streams of considerable size, whose course, in many instances, is marked by the line of funnel-shaped sinks where tho sand above tho rocky strata has filtered down through abrasions of tho rocks, and has been carried off by tho current beneath, leaving tho sinks, at tho bottom of which water is always present, and in many of which fish are

abundant. Many of these extensive fountains are mineral—sulphur, iron, magnesia, lime, etc., being the
constituents. There are but few extensive marshes in
the State. At the sources on the summits are often found
savannas, covering many acres, but they do not, like the
marshes and savannas in many other countries, consist of
deep alluvial deposits, which have been brought down from
higher elevations, because these are the summits themselves
from which the water supply of the rivers come. This is a
peculiarity in Florida. That larger area on the lower end of
the peninsula, and known as the Everglades, and covered by
water, is by many supposed to be marshy; but such is not
the fact, for it is simply a shallow lake, elevated above the
ocean some ten or more feet, surrounded by a rocky rim, with
a sandy and rocky bottom, containing clear, fresh water,
which is discharged through fissures or apertures in the rocky
rim into Key Biscayne Bay, and through outlets on the west
side into the Gulf. At the north of the Everglades is Lake
Okeeckobee, the largest body of fresh water in the interior of
the State. It is fed by the Kissimee river, whose source is
in the same savanna or summit level which is the source of
the St. John's river. Its outlet is into the Everglades. Interspersed through this savana, and at the head of the
Oclawaha river, are numerous lakes, which, by modifying and
equalizing the temperature, render the country around their
borders peculiarly adapted to the culture of oranges and
other tropical fruits, while at the same time the residents
enjoy good health both summer and winter.

Rainy Season.—Our so-called rainy season, though sufficiently marked to warrant the designation most years, is not
always so well defined. It generally embraces a period of
about sixty days, and ordinarily commences about the middle

of June, and terminates about the middle of August, but it oscillates from May to September. Sometimes the rainy season apparently commences, and perhaps daily showers will occur regularly for one or two weeks or more, and then, perhaps, weeks of clear, settled weather will be interpolated, and the rainy season will come on again and continue, so that about the usual complement of rainy days will occur. During the rainy season the rain is by no means continuous, but comes in showers of from a half to one hour or more in continuance, and between the hours of from 1 to 4 P. M., sometimes, but not always, attended with thunder and lightning.

Before the shower, the atmosphere may be hot and sultry, but afterwards the sun shines out, the air is pure, cool, and refreshing. The showers generally come with such regularity that they need not interrupt business, labor or pleasure, only during their continuance, for timely preparation to avoid them can be made if desired.

Health.—As to the subject of miasmata, we have nothing in Florida to render it the cause of disease more than in any country north of us, where new soil is turned up to the air and sun. The heat which we have does not seem to generate anything of the kind here. Florida is, happily, free from many of the diseases which are prevalent elsewhere.

WEST INDIES.

The name West Indies is usually given to the vast archipelago of about one thousand islands, lying between North and South America, extending in two irregular lines which unite at Hayti, from the peninsulas of Yucatan and Florida to the mouth of the Orinoco. They enclose the Caribbean Sea, dividing it from the Gulf of Mexico, and from the Atlantic Ocean. They lie between latitude 10° and 28° North, longitude 57° and 85° West, and are divided into four groups. *First*—The Bahamas, about 500 in number, being a continuation of the coral formation, extending towards Hayti. *Second*—The Greater Antilles. *Third*—The Lesser Antilles. *Fourth*—The Leeward Islands.

The following figures give the area of several of the larger islands and groups, their population, and the population of their capital cities. Hayti, 11,718 square miles; population, 560,000; capital, Port-au-Prince; population, 30,000. Dominica, 17,172 square miles; population, 200,000; capital, San Domingo; population, 15,000. Spanish West Indies, 47,130 square miles; population, 1,832,062; capital, Havana, Cuba; population, 130,000; San Juan, Porto Rico, population, 30,000. British West Indies, 13,414 square miles; population, 820,792; capitals, Spanish Town, Jamaica; population, 6,000; Nassau, Bahama Islands, population, 7,000; Port-au-Spain, Trinidad, population, 12,000. French West Indies, 1,691 square miles; population, 256,511; capital, Point-au-Pitre; population, 12,000. Netherlands West Indies, 413 square miles; population, 38,600; capital, Curacoa; population, 7,000. Danish West Indies, 110 square miles, population, 37,137; capital, Christanstead; population, 5,500, and Saint Thomas, population, 10,000. Swedish West Indies, 35 Square miles; population, 18,000; capital, Gustavia; population, 10,000; Venezuelian West Indies 500 square miles; population, 20,000.

The surface of the West India Islands, is very diversified. The Bahamas, are low and flat, and entirely of a Coraline formation. The Antilles, greater and lesser are volcanic, and form the peaks of a mountain chain, continuous with the North East range of Venezuela, and rising in Cuba, Hayti and

Jamaica, into summits of from 5,000 to 7,000 feet high, and
in many of the lesser Antilles, to the hight of from 4,000 to
5,000 feet. In Saint Vincjent and Guadaloupe, there are
active volcanoes, and Hayti and Jamacia, are subject to
earthquakes. The Bahamas, being low, are sultry and hot,
though for a part of the day, the sea breezes temper tho
heat. The more mountainous islands have a temperate and
delightful climate; especially so, in the highlands. The
Islands abound in minerals. The copper mines of Cuba, are
among the most extensive on the Globe. Gold, silver, alum,
copperas, and excellent coal are found on the same Island.
Gold, silver, copper, tin, iron and rock salt in Hayti. Lead,
copper and salt in Jamaica. Gold, copper, iron, lead and
coal in Porto Rico. Asphaltum and coal oil in Trinidad, and
salt in the Bahamas.

The characteristic feature, of the botany in the West
Indies is the great predominance of ferns and archedaceous
plants. The forests furnish mahogany, lignum-vitae, granna-
dilla, rose-wood and other woods of great value for ornamental
and other purposes.

The fruits are mostly tropical in their character, and many
of them are of excellent quality. The pineapple, cocoanut,
pomegranate, mango-guava, orange, lemon, lime, bread fruit,
and banana, many of them of numerous varieties abound.

Of spices, drugs and dyestuffs, indigo, ginger, pepper
aloes, sassafras, cochineal, logwood, etc., are the principal.
Maize is largely cultivated in most of the islands, while tobacco, coffee and sugar are staples in several, and cotton is
considerably cultivated.

The animals, birds and reptiles are those of the semi-
tropics. On two of the islands only, St. Vincent and Trini-

dad, are any of the original inhabitants found, and but very few on them—only a few isolated families.

GEOGRAPHICAL AND POLITICAL DIVISIONS OF THE WEST INDIES.

Antilles.—The Antilles are divided into two groups. The Greater Antilles, including the four large islands, viz.: Cuba, San Domingo, Jamaica and Porto Rico. The Lesser Antilles, sometimes called the Caribbean Islands, number between 700 and 800, though some of them are mere islets.

Geographically, the Antilles extend in a broken line from latitude 10° N., longitude 60° 54 W. along the southern coast of Florida, nearly to Yucatan, from which it is separated by the channel of Yucatan, with a general trend W. 40° N. through a course of 1,500 miles.

Leeward Islands.—Those islands lying north of 15° N. latitude are known as the Leeward Islands.

Windward Islands.—Those islands lying south of 15° N. latitude are known as the Windward Islands.

Virgin Islands.—Are those islands lying east of Porto Rico, viz. : Barbadoes, Antigua, Dominica, Saint Lucie, Trinidad, Saint Vincent, Barbuda, Grenada, Tobago and Saint Thomas.

Politically the Antilles are divided as follows :

Independent.—Hayti.

English.—Jamaica, Antigua, Barbadoes, Barbuda, Anguilla, Dominica, Grenada, Grenadines (a part of the Virgin group), Montseratt, Nevis, Saint Christopher, Saint Lucie, Saint Vincent, Tobago and Trinidad.

Spanish.—Cuba and Porto Rico.

Venezuelian.—Margoritta, Lestigas, Tortuga, Blanguilla, Orchilla and Roca.

French.—Guadaloupe, Martinique, Marie Galante, All Saintes, Deseada and part of Saint Martin.

Dutch.—Part of Saint Martin, Aves, Buen Ayre, Curacoa, Aruba, Saba and Saint Eustatius.

Danish.—Saint Thomas, Saint Johns and Saint Croix.

Swedish.—Saint Bartholomew.

There are very many other islands, the nationalities of which are the same as the larger contiguous islands herein enumerated.

The entire area of the Antilles is 150,000 square miles, and the population something more than 4,000,000.

Commerce.—The present commerce of the Antilles is $260,000,000.

AMERICAN SHIPPING PLYING BETWEEN THE UNITED STATES AND THE CARIBBEAN SEA.

The following is a copy of a letter from the Secretary of the Treasury relative to the commerce of the United States, with the islands and mainlands of the Caribbean Sea :

TREASURY DEPARTMENT,
WASHINGTON, D. C., Sept. 5, 1874.

SIR:

* * I enclose herewith a statement of the steamships of the United States making trips between the Atlantic ports and ports of the West India Islands and countries bordering on the Caribbean Sea and the Gulf of Mexico. The statement shows the respective routes, the ports touched at on the voyage, the names of the several lines, the tonnage of each, and the number of trips made each year.

I have the honor to be, sir,
Your obedient servant,
B. H. BRISTOW, Secretary.

8

Statement of American steamers making trips between Atlantic ports of the United States and ports of the West India Islands and countries bordering on the Caribbean Sea and the Gulf of Mexico, for the year ending July 31, 1874 :

Philadelphia and Southern Mail Steamship Company.

Termini, Philadelphia and New Orleans ; touches at Havana Whole number steamers, 2 ; total tonnage, 2,606 ; whole number trips, 24.

Baltimore, New Orleans and Havana Steamship Company.

Termini, Baltimore and New Orleans ; touches at Key West and Havana. Whole number steamers, 2 ; total tonnage, 2,125 ; whole number trips, 22.

New. Orleans, Florida and Havana Steamship Company.

Termini, New Orleans and Havana ; touches at Cedar Key and Key West. Whole number steamers, 2 ; total tonnage, 1,012 ; round trip, 10 to 14 days.

New York and Mexican Main Line.

Termini, New York and Vera Cruz ; touches at Havana, Cuba, Progresso, Mexico, and Nassau, N. P. Whole number steamers, 6 ; total tonnage, 8,056 ; whole number of trips, 76.

Clyde Line.

Termini, New York and Havana ; touches —. Whole number steamers, 5 ; total tonnage, 7,151 ; whole number trips, 43.

Mallory's (Occasional.)

Termini, New York and Havana ; touches —. Whole number steamers, 3 ; total tonnage, 8,584 ; whole number trips. 4.

Lunt Brothers Line.

Termini, New York and Hamilton ; touches at Saint Thomas. Whole number steamers, 3 : total tonnage, 2,341 ; whole number trips, 15.

Samana Bay Company.

Termini, New York and San Domingo ; touches —. Whole number steamers, 1; total tonnage, 800; whole number trips, 7.

Wm. P. Clyde & Company.

Termini, New York and Samana ; touches at San Domingo and Porto Plata. Whole number steamers, 2 ; total tonnage, 1,317; whole number trips, 2.

New York and West India Steamship Company.

Termini, New York and Port-au-Prince ; touches —. Whole number steamers, 2 ; total tonnage, 1,494; whole number trips, 15.

Cromwell Line.

Termini, New York and Havana; touches —. Whole number steamers, 3 ; total tonnage, 4,061; whole number trips, 5.

W. H. Thorne and Others.

Termini, New York and Ponce, Porto Rico ; touches — Whole number steamers, 1 ; total tonnage, 204 ; whole number trips, 1.

United States and Brazil Mail Steamship Company.

Termini, New York and Rio Janeiro ; touches at Saint Thomas. Whole number steamers, 3 ; total tonnage, 7,801 ; whole number trips, 11.

Pacific Mail Steamship Line.

Termini, New York and Aspinwall; touches —. Whole number steamers, 8 ; total tonnage, 18,924 ; whole number trips, 31.

Morgan Line.

Termini, Galveston and Havana ; touches —. Whole number steamships, 4 ; total tonnage, 3,693 ; whole number. trips, 13 each.

Whole number trips.................. 370
Whole number steamships.............. 47
Total tonnage.....................65,169

EDWARD YOUNG,

Chief Bureau Statistics.

NOTE.—The above statement is abridged from the original letter from the Bureau Statistics.

European Steamships Trading with the West Indies and South America.

The following summary of the steamers that were making regular trips in 1874, from the countries designated, to the West Indies and the eastern coast of Central and South America, is taken from the Hamberger Boersen Halle, a financial paper, published in Hamburg, Germany. The article does not state that all the steamers in this trade are given.

The summary is as follows:

ENGLAND.—82 steamers, registering 118,351 tons.

GERMANY.—13 steamers, registering 26,617 tons. .

ITALY.—6 steamers, registering 8,780 tons.

SPAIN.—3 steamers, registering 5,200 tons.

HOLLAND.—3 steamers, registering 4,500 tons.

Total—107 steamers, registering 163,448 tons.

Adding to the above the steamers from the United States, trading with the same countries we have the following:

EUROPE.—107 steamers, registering 163,448 tons.

UNITED STATES.—47 steamers, registering 65,169 tons.

Total—154 steamers, registering 228,617 tons.

Nothing is said here of the vast number of sailing vessels, the number and tonnage of which no reliable data could be obtained; trading with these same countries. But the aggregate number and tonnage must very largely exceed those of the steamers. The freights carried by the sailing vessels must exceed that carried by steamers manyfold.

RUSSIAN RAILWAYS.

The paragraph below, is inserted, to show that in all sections of the world, the large grain carrying roads, and those upon which, there is much pleasure travel, are profitable. It is the same in Russia as in the United States. In both of these branches of traffic, the road now under contemplation, will receive a very great patronage.

"The Russian Government," "has just issued a report on the railway traffic during the year, from which are taken the following facts. In the month of March, 1874, the railways of Russia comprised 15,380 versts, or about 11,000 miles. The gross receipts during that month amounted to 11,955,007 roubles, while in February, 1873, the receipts were 9,306,409 roubles. The increase was, therefore, 2,648,598 roubles, or 28 1-3 per cent. For the first quarter of the present year—from the 1st of January to the 1st of April, 1874—the gross income of the 44 lines now in operation was 33,443,839 roubles, against 25,969,899 roubles received during the first quarter of 1873. This increase is satisfactory enough but an examination of the results obtained by the different lines discloses beside that the traffic on some of them is increasing with giant strides. The average receipts per verst during the quarter were 2,177 roubles, and the average increase on the quarter of 1873 amounted to 12½ per cent. per verst. It is impossible not to be struck by the marvelous development of traffic exhibited by the return from several lines. The greatest percentage is shown by the Riga-Boldera and Constantinople lines ; but these are only of local interest.

We, therefore, proceed to the Ribinsk, Warsaw, Brest and
Baltic lines, showing respectively an increase of 98 per cent.
65 per cent. and 64 per cent. The first is of great importance for the transportation of grain from the Volga to St.
Petersburg. All the wheat shipped from this capital and
consumed in it notoriously come from the tracts near the
Volga and the Ribinsk line was specially constructed to facilitate this transport. The increase in the traffic shows that
the native merchants have not been slow in availing themselves of the accommodation. The Warsaw-Brest line is
part of the great network which connects the capital of
Poland with Moscow and all the richest portions of Central
and South Russia. The great resources of this region are
only now beginning to be appreciated, and the traffic of this
trunk line is likely to be on the increase for some time. It
is very certain, too, that as it becomes known to foreign
traders that Revel and Baltishport remain free from ice long
after the closing of the port of St. Petersburg, the trade of
those places will grow greatly to the advantage of this railway. The Riga Dunabourg line, with its increase of 40 per
cent. again shows the natural development of trade on an
old-established highway, and it is extremely satisfactory to
see that almost all the great trunk lines show an augmenta-
tion averaging 20 per cent.

THE DARIEN SHIP CANAL.

Looking to the future, it is well to call attention, more ex-
plicity here, to the prospective construction of the Darien
Ship Canal. The road in contemplation will more nearly, by
several hundred miles, approach this work, when it shall be
undertaken, than any other road, or inland route of travel.

and commerce. All steamers, and sailing vessels, traversing the Gulf Stream, to and from the canal, will pass within 30 miles of Turtle Harbor, and 40 miles of Key West, and as a result, much traffic will be concentrated upon the road, from vessels putting in at these ports, While a large commerce seek its passage through the canal from the interior of the United States via the line of this road.

To illustrate how great the traffic will be through the canal when completed we make the following extract from the report of Commander Thomas O. Selfridge, Commander of the Darien Expedition.

"The trade through the canal would be ample at the expiration of a year to meet the interest of the debt raised; and in a few years a sinking fund could be created, to take up the whole amount loaned."

Table showing amount of trade that would pass through the canal the first year. Compiled from statistics for the years 1867 and 1869.

UNITED STATES.

Countries Traded with	Imports and Exports, 1869.	Tonnage.
Dutch East Indies..	$2,080,031	13,382
British Australia and New Zealand	809,037	44,624
British East Indies.............	9,452,214	107,977
Half Mexico......	₹5,999,997	72,930
Half Central America	2,109,778	41,520
Chili..	3,272,467	49,078
Sandwich Islands.....	2,083,484	56,603
Peru....	3,059,755	78,429
China	25,584,853	107,884
Half New Granada	5,186,025	308,220
California.......	13,000,000	160,000
Value of cargoes.	$72,617,611	$1,040,548
Value ships $50 per ton........	52,027,400	
Total value ships and cargoes..	$124,645,011	

ENGLAND.

Countries Traded with.	Imports and Exports.	Tonnage.
Half Mexico....................	$3,014,005	$22,401
Half Central America............	2,642,650	7,625
Half New Grenada..............	8,613,995	11,019
Chili.	35,004,090	220,771
Peru and Ecuador	26,701,825	212,126
China........................	85,975,900	197,288
Java..........................	6,812,765	30,703

Singapore	17,813,505	123,436
Australia and New Zealand	67,475,780	261,815
California and Pacific Islands	14,476,700	129,348
Value of cargoes	$268,531,115	$1,219,762 •
Value ships $50 per ton	60,988,100	•

Total value ships and cargoes...$329,519,215

FRANCE.—The trade of France for the year 1865 amounted to a total value of ships and cargoes of $60,839,135. Tonnage 165,259.

It is estimated by the statistics of 1857 that the total tonnage that would seek the canal would be 3,094,070 tons. Allowing this to be about correct, the canal would have a revenue from

3,064,070 tons at $2.50 per tons	$7,735,075
100,000 passengers at $10 per head	$1,000,000
Total revenue, first year	$8,735,175

During the construction of this canal, which is now a fixed port, in the not distant future, the existence of a railroad to Key West with an abundance of steamship connections would result in saving many millions to whosoever should build it, and directly and indirectly add many millions to the commerce of the United States.

NICARAGUA SHIP CANAL.

Cost of construction taken from the report of Commander E. P. LULL, U. S. Navy, Commanding Nicaragua Surveying Expedition.

The following estimates are from the report of A. G. Menocal.

" Estimate of the cost of constructing a Ship Canal from the Atlantic to the Pacific Ocean, across the Isthmus in the

State of Nicaragua, upon the line surveyed by the Nicaraguan Surveying Expedition.

The total distance from the harbor of Brito, on the Pacific, to the harbor of Graytown, or San Juan del Norte, upon the Atlantic, is 181.26 statute miles which may be divided as follows :

Inland Canal, Western Division, from the mouth of Rio del Medio, at the Lake, to the Harbor of Brito................................. 16.33 miles

Middle Division, comprising the Lake navigation from the mouth of Rio del Medio to Fort San Carlos......... .... 56.50 miles

Eastern Division, from San Carlos at the Lake, to Graytown, slack water navigation, 63.02 ; inland canal, 45.41 = ... 108.43 miles

TOTAL COST.

Western Division.........................	$21,680,777
Middle Division.........	715,658
Eastern Division................ ....:..	25,020,914
Harbor of Brito, (improvement)..............	2,337,739
Harbor of Graytown, (improvement)..........	2,822,630
Total................................. ...	$52,577,718
Add 25 per cent. for contingencies	13,144,429
Grand Total........................... ...	$65,722,147

The report from Commander Lull, from which the foregoing extract is taken, was transmitted by the Secretary of the Navy to Congress, on the 16th of June, 1874.

MAIL FACILITIES.

By this route the mails will be carried from New York to Cuba daily, in sixty hours, and to Hayti and San Domingo in thirty-six hours from the terminus of the road. Mails for Central and South America will be from four to six days. The mails from all cities south and west of New York, which are now sent to Cuba via New York, will reach their destination in proportionately less time. The great through mails between the United States and all the West Indies, Central and South America, must go by this line. The advantage thus accruing will be incalculable.

BUSINESS SESSION OF THE POSTAL CONVENTION.
MEMORIAL TO CONGRESS.

FORTRESS MONROE, Va., July 26, 1877.—The Chairman of the Committee on Business, submitted resolutions favoring increased postal facilities for Southern cities, the establishment of steam communication between convenient Southern ports and Rio Janeiro, Havana and Aspinwall, and that the Congress of the United States and Postal Department are respectfully requested to afford aid and encouragement to the above designated enterprises by means of liberal mail contracts and such appropriate legislation as may be consistent with the constitutional powers and policy of the Government.

Accompanying the resolutions was a memorial to Congress setting forth the needs of the South, and asking that the following measures be provided for :

Sixth.—The establishment on some substantial basis of the mail contracts of steamship line between Southern seaports and ports of South America, Central America and the West Indies.

The report was adopted unanimously.

The Postmaster General in his report, dated Washington, D. C., November 27, 1876, says :

"The United States postage on mails conveyed to and from the West Indies, Panama, Central America, Brazil, Mexico, Bermuda, Nova Scotia, New Granada, Venezuela, and Honolulu, at the reduced rates established from July 1, 1875, amounted to $119,617.68, and the cost of the sea conveyance thereof was $45,436.79."

The paragraphs below are from the message of President Grant, of December 7, 1874. The subject matter is applicable here, as showing that the attention of Congress was called by the President to the development of commerce with the countries to which he alludes, and which this road will tend so much to develop, as well as to the necessity of increasing our steamship service :

"The use of the navy in time of peace might be further utilized by a direct authorization of the employment of naval vessels in explorations and surveys of the supposed navigable waters of other nationalities on this continent, especially the tributaries of the two great rivers of South America, the Oronoco and the Amazon. Nothing prevents, under existing laws, such exploration, except that expenditures must be made in such expeditions beyond those usually provided for in the appropriations. The field designated is unquestionably one of interest and one capable of large development of commercial interests advantageous to the people reached, and to those who may establish relations with them.

"A revival of ship building, and particularly iron steamship building, is of vast importance to our national prosperity. The United States is now paying over one hundred millions per annum for freights and passage on foreign ships, to be carried abroad and expended in the employment and support of other people. Beyond a fair percentage of what should go to foreign vessels, estimating on the tonnage and travel of each respectively, it is to be regretted that this disparity in the carrying trade exists, and, to correct it, I would be willing to see a great departure from the usual course of government in supporting what might usually be termed private enterprise. I would not suggest, as a remedy, direct subsidy to American steamship lines, but I would suggest the direct offer of ample compensation for carrying the mails between Atlantic seaboard cities and the continent, on American owned and American built steamers, and would extend the liberality to vessels carrying the mails to South American States, and to Central America and Mexico, and would pursue the same policy from our pacific seaports to foreign seaports on the Pacific. It might be demanded that vessels built for this service should come up to a standard fixed by legislation in tonnage, speed and all other qualities, looking to the possibility of government requiring them at some time for war purposes. The right also of taking possession of them in such emergency should be guarded. I offer these suggestions believing them worthy of consideration in all seriousness, affecting all sections and all interests alike. If anything better can be done to direct the country into a course of general prosperity, no one will be more ready than I to second the plan."

————

PRODUCTS OF THE SOIL OF THE UNITED STATES.

As an illustration of how large a proportion of the entire productions of the United States this Railway commands as shown in the accompaning papers we give the total products of the soil of the United States, as compiled by Hon. S. Shellabarger, from the census of the United States for 1870, and published 1874.

"The total products of the soil including farms, orchards and gardens, was in 1870, $2,515,592,753. In that year we produced of wheat, 287,745,626 bushels; of rye, 16,918,795 bushels; of indian corn, 760,944.549 bushels; of oats, 288,107,157 bushels; of barley, 29,761,503 bushels; of buckwheat, 9,821,721 bushels; of rice; 73,365,021 pounds; of tobacco, 262,735,341 pounds, and of cotton, 3,011,996 bales. The total of cereals in 1870, was 1,629,027.6 bushels. The aggregate of the products of our manufactures in 1870, was $4,232,-325,442.

COMMERCIAL IMPORTANCE OF THE ROAD.

This route brings the railroad system of the United States withing 90 miles of the railroads of Cuba. The commerce of the United States with the West Indies constitutes nearly 11 per cent. of the entire commerce of the country, for the greater proportion of which is with Cuba. The commerce of the United States with the countries that will be tributary to this road is 20 per cent. of the commerce of the country.

These facts are established by the following official table accompanying a message of the President to the Senate, dated January 16, 1871, transmitting papers relative to the proposed annexation of San Domingo :

Relative Commercial Importance of the West Indies in the Commerce of the United States for the year ending 30th June, 1870 ; compiled from returns in the Statistical Bureau of the Treasury Department.

	Imports.	Exports.	Total.
Cuba	$54,056,415	$17,412,781	$71,469,196
Porto Rico	8,183,240	2,955,324	11,138,573
	$62,239,664	$20,368,105	$82,607,769
Hayti and S. Domingo.	979,965	2,801,333	3,780,988
Danish West Indies...	628,870	1,488,399	2,117,269
Dutch West Indies and Dutch Guiana	731,973	970,937	2,702,910
French Pos.in America.	467,389	1,167,190	1,634,579
British West Indies...	6,572,555	8,279,627	14,852,182
	$71,620,106	$35,075,591	$106,595,697
Dominion of Canada..	$39,507,842	$23,297,296	$62,805,138
All other British Possessions in America..	1,581,959	3,552,028	5,133,987
	$41,039,801	$26,849,324	$67,939,125
Mexico	$13,099,131	$5,875,396	$18,974,427
Central America	775,673	1,161,695	1,897,368
Colombia	5,206,190	4,791,620	9,797,810
Peru	2,557,833	3,793,185	6,351,018
Chili	773,082	2,245,809	3,019,491
Argentine Republic....	6,414,669	2,479,437	8,894,106
Uruguay	1,630,400	1,199,237	2,829,637
Brazil	25,178,959	5,817,846	30,993,805
Venezuela.	2,037,312	1,324,325	3,361,637
	$57,430,749	$28,688,550	$86,119,299
Total America	$170,140,656	$90,613,465	$260,754,120

RECAPITULATION.

	Imports.	Exports.	Total.
Commerce with West Indies...............	$71,620,106	$35,075,591	$106,695,697
Mexico, Central and S. America.	57,430,749	28,688,550	186,179,299
British Possessions in North America.....	41,089,801	26,849,324	67,039,125
	$170,140,656	$90,613,465	$260,754,129
Tot'l commerce of U.S.	$462,377,587	$529,159,302	$991,896,889

Commerce with the West Indies forms nearly eleven per cent; the West Indies, Mexico, Central and South America, nearly twenty per cent. of total commerce of United States; and all British Possessions on this Continent, only six and three-quarter per cent. of total.

This 20 per cent. of the total commerce of the United States this route will bring directly to our doors, cutting off from two to four days in transportation. Commerce now demands speed. Time is money. The traffic of the roads now running parallel with the seaboard and with the Ohio, the Mississippi and the great lakes, and that of the Pacific Roads, demonstrate this. While bulky and slow freights must continue to be transported by water, an annual commerce of $260,000,000 directly south of the terminus of this route imperatively demands these additional facilities.

But it must be remembered, in considering whether such a rail route can compete with the water route, that the water route practically carries the products of the American tropics far to the northeast, to be afterward retransported to the south and west by rail. This route, on the contrary, brings all the Southern States into direct and close relations with the West Indies, with which their commerce will be carried on directly, without the immense additional cost of transporting it from 500 to 1,000 miles to the north and thence back again to the South. So, also, the Western States will be but little further from Havana, either in distance or time, from New York, and fully one-third of the time and cost of transportation between the Western States and the West Indies will be saved.

The opening of these close relations with the West Indies will rapidly develop a greatly enlarged market for our productions, and will turn to this country a much greater proportion of the vast West India° commerce that properly belongs to us, but is now diverted to Europe by subsidized steamship lines.

On the commercial importance of the line, reference is made to other official tables of the commerce of the United States given elsewhere.

STATEMENTS

Showing the value of Chief Articles imported into the United States from the West Indies, Mexico, Central America, Venezuela and New Granada ; also the Chief Articles exported from the United States to the same countries during the fiscal years ending June 30th, 1865 to 1870, inclusive :

IMPORTS.

COUNTRIES.	Coffee.	Sugar.	Molasses.	Tobacco.	Fruits.	Dyewoods.	Spices.	Cabinet Wood.	Specie.	Hides and Skins.
	$	$	$	$	$	$	$	$	$	$
WEST INDIES.										
Swedish W. I.	267	18,485	22,668	....	3,251	....	104	....	16,672	1,362
Danish "	19,713	1,179,823	1,128,474	949,063	1,041	1,108	5,706	10,965	261,020	79,823
Dutch "	79,217	579,974	126,847	3,095	5,436	299,040	386	41,017	608,761	884,659
British "	1,046,458	9,303,025	4,560,556	164,597	710,804	1,664,739	271,023	149,128	1,116,411	125,166
French "	....	756,693	68,702	....	14,867	....	....	....	3,100	3,100
Cuba	272,393	196,998,497	46,000,563	15,994,846	1,377,005	129,777	22,263	861,218	4,254,705	137,766
Porto Rico	143,418	27,810,802	9,602,157	2,714	101,687	12,187	72	10,141	10,129	18,916
Hayti & S. Domingo	2,689,346	1,208,046	9,819	9,368	4,886	1,577,034	127	347,336	159,833	94,072
Mexico	347,883	193,944	12,519	14,606	105,113	954,573	238,879	640,586	21,917,281	3,230,731
Central Republics	2,912,808	474,623	1,181	411	17,355	79,884	....	59,061	39,430	347,645
Venezuela	8,214,214	47,016	2,829	1,337	8,492	164,560	....	16,251	1,151,564	2,389,617
New Granada	833,995	57,269	268	388,164	99,490	122,796	215	23,587	2,053,478	2,160,277
Total	$16,459,702	$237,026,387	$60,436,443	$17,318,263	$2,446,221	$4,796,297	$538,886	$2,178,231	$36,391,244	$9,469,934

Exports of Domestic Products in the six years from 1865 to 1870, inclusive.

COUNTRIES.	Butter.	Manufa'res of Wood.	Cheese.	Drugs.	Fish, P'kled & Smoked.	Wheat Flour.	Coal.	Lard and Pork.	Petroleum.	Manufa'res of Cotton.
WEST INDIES.	$	$	$	$	$	$	$	$	$	$
Swedish W. I.	511	26,456	1,515	212	172	16,725		603	49	
Danish "	197,580	19,811	32,922	69,615	149,064	1,823,956	69,741	475,925	791,783	49,294
Dutch "	103,384	384,212	4,441	26,947	35,779	1,925,389	27,119	1,110,340	60,588	33,600
British "	727,905	18,907	357,928	315,697	325,031	16,088,560	39,392	5,595,315	941,537	269,833
French "	12,448	949,864	2,565	5,486	125,653	913,941		626,994	95,461	9,893
Cuba	846,384	243,019	185,686	926,910	355,004	3,943,085	264,962	10,374,473	2,298,469	817,020
Porto Rico	259,885	205,506	260,605	131,967	384,723	2,950,961	7,115	2,236,272	296,748	21,729
Hayti & S. Domingo	347,939	681,976	192,122	99,553	3,175,345	4,935,594	84,000	5,446,188	196,384	636,177
Mexico	191,439	20,876	215,363	708,863	32,301	4,364,976	351,331	975,871	935,763	5,827,313
Central Republics.	46,348	27,860	16,419	46,064	16,141	390,267	223,546	68,390	16,974	306,725
Venezuela	163,554	34,960	16,419	184,296	32,094	1,805,717	4,627	754,542	457,386	61,022
New Grenada	655,764	131,191	92,375	997,508	116,004	722,241	940,235	768,627	433,844	2,706,967
Total	$3,573,731	$2,683,149	$1,329,277	$8,525,090	$4,761,513	$38,883,414	$2,012,036	$29,325,581	$6,445,396	$10,738,577

Exports of Foreign Products from 1865 to 1870, inclusive.

COUNTRIES.	Tea.	Drugs.	Fire Crackers (1865 to 1868).	Fish.	Perfumery.	Rice.	Soap (1865 to 1868)	Opium.	Sugar Refined.
WEST INDIES.	$	$	$	$	$	$	$	• $	$
Swedish W.I.	4,861	2,369	2,216	25,610	7,985	1,218	10,543		18,829
Danish "	445	169	5,465	37,405	1,968		4,635	1,211	13,309
Dutch "	27,649	14,493	805	30,989	6,026	29,716	13	5,493	33,074
British "	17,329			2,939		34,571			130
French "	22,620	169,621	7,255	35,214	56,739	352,252	8,302	1,022,381	2,800
Cuba	1,596	13,577	5,739	20,899	9,475	225,760	8,107		232
Porto Rico	353	2,922	1,030	402,004	2,974	195,795	21,613	60	278,142
Hayti and San Domingo	50,182	296,437	16,777	73,884	14,303	109,542	28,570	35,078	182,498
Mexico	11,613	3,075	1,021	4,813		4,496	96		56,613
Central Republic	436	14,399	10,377	1,154	4,285	16,682	4,881	98	6,605
Venezuela	139,719	92,754	3,908	4,430	12,158	38,444	6,957	122,055	370,386
New Grenada									
Total	$176,764	$519,806	$63,583	$1,039,641	$116,513	$1,007,484	$93,617	$1,186,396	$962,618

BUREAU OF STATISTICS, Jan. 31st, 1871.   EDWARD YOUNG, Chief of Bureau.

SUMMARY.

Countries.	Total Exports.	Total Imports.	Total Commerce.
Swedish West Indies*..	$19,817	$62,729	$82,546
Danish " ...	3,743,062	3,636,826	7,379,888
Dutch " ...	2,434,625	2,628,432	5,053,087
British " ...	25,194,868	18,910.267	44,105,135
French " ...	1,766,309	843,352	2,609,661
Cuba.................	22,598,392	266,009,945	288,608,337
Porto Rico...... ,.....	7,021,029	36,612,183	43,633,212
Hayti and San Domingo	16,503,714	4,999,968	21,503,682
Mexico,..............	15,004,464	32,954,217	47,958,681
Central Republics.....	1,304,411	3,930,290	5,334,701
Venezuela............	3,602,934	11,880,880	15,483,814
New Grenada.........	8,201,567	7,189,418	15,390,985
Total..........	$107,385,522	398,658,507	497,043,729

Thus the commerce, in chief articles only, with those countries that lie nearest the terminus of the line, was, $497,043,729.

Passenger Traffic.—The advantage for transferring through passengers between the United [States and the West Indies, and all the countries to the South, which this route will offer above all others, and are too apparent to need argument. The saving of from two to four days' time, and 1,245 miles of ocean travel, will bring the United States into as intimate relations with Cuba and the West Indies as we now are with the States west of the Missouri. Indeed, the distance from Washington to Havana by this route is the same as from Washington to Omaha.

COMMERCE OF THE UNITED STATES WITH THE SEVERAL PORTS OF THE CARRIBBEAN SEA.

It being the intention, and embraced within the plans of this Railway Company, to reach by its own steamers, as authorized by its charter, every part of the Caribbean Sea, both on the islands and on the main land, a letter was addressed to the Assistant Secretary of the Treasury, Hon. F. A. Sawyer, requesting that a statement be furnished showing the extent of the commerce of the United States with those ports during the fiscal year of 1872. The letter of the Assistant Secretary is as follows, to wit;

TREASURY DEPARTMENT, }
WASHINGTON, *May,* 2d, 1873. }

DEAR SIR : I have the honor to acknowledge the receipt of your letter of the 20th inst., asking for information in regard to the trade between the United States and the West India Islands and the countries bordering on the Caribbean Sea, during the fiscal year 1872, and, in response thereto, transmit herewith a statement prepared by the Bureau of Statistics giving the information desired, as far as practicable.

Very respectfully yours,

FREDERICK A. SAWYER,

Ass't Secretary.

STATEMENT showing the Trade of the United States with Islands and Countries bordering on the Carribbean Sea during the year ending June 30, 1872 :

Countries.	Imports.	Domestic Exports.	Foreign Exports.
United States of Colombia	$6,589,449	$4,495,258	$181,501
Venzuela	4,474,201	2,178,388	32,052
Central American States	1,609,044	1,406,855	71,060
British West Indies	9,550,347	8,658,637	138,429

Cuba	67,720,205	13,168,958	1,570,010
Porto Rico	11,328,681	2,643,155	190,927
Dutch West Indies and Guiana	1,067,564	789,255	24,946
Hayti	1,080,791	2,737,488	204,373
San Domingo	437,160	589,259	39,859
Danish West Indies	768,167	1,071,504	68,116
French Possessions in America	2,290,963	1,460,746	37,298

$$\$106,916,572 \quad \$39,199,503 \quad \$2,570,571$$
$$\cdot 39,159,903$$
$$106,916\,572$$

Total Commerce.......................... $148,686,646

EDWARD YOUNG

Chief of Bureau.

The foregoing statement does not include British or French Guiana nor any of the commerce that would come over the Panama Railway from the west coast of the continent, which, on shipment from the eastern termini of that road, is but a few hours' run from Key West and this Railway. Thus more speedy and quick transportation will be secured, and the dangers of the passage of the Florida reefs as well as high rates of insurance will be avoided.

The statement of Commissioner Young does not include the commerce of Yucatan and southern Mexico, which is large and rapidly increasing.

All of this traffic will find its quickest, safest and cheapest route by the steamers and over the road of this Company.

There cannot be a doubt but that so large a proportion of this commerce will pass over this road that its financial success will be secured from the time it reaches a harbor at the south end of the Peninsula of Florida.

FOREIGN COMMERCE OF THE UNITED STATES WITH THE FOLLOWING
COUNTRIES DURING THE YEAR 1874.

	Imports from.	Exports to,
Great Britain	$168,718,742	$379,341,890
France	60,653,838	50,212,296
Germany	40,756,468	64,654,012
Canada	35,308,348	40,875,154
Brazil	43,327,332	8,551,997
China and Japan	24,927,008	3,195,262
British North America	371,755	1,647,396
British West Indies	4,182,377	8,057,345
Other West Indies	4,186,237	3,091,830
East Indies	21,574,229	1,466,832
Mexico	12,091,998	6,249,163
Holland and Belgium	8,782,054	28,624,368
Cuba and Porto Rico	82,372,509	24,607,561
All others	70,116,231	81,944,410
Total	$577,369,711	$702,529,855

MILITARY AND NAVAL.

The map shows the fact that the terminus of the road commands the straits at Florida at the narrowest point, and places that point in railway connection with the rest of the country. It becomes thus a more important work for the defense of the country than any work of whatever nature now in contemplation can possibly be.

EFFECT ON POLITICAL RELATIONS.

A Bond of Peace.—The West Indies gravitate toward the United States. The Cuban insurgents have been asking recognition, with a view to annexation. San Domingo has asked a participation in our nationality. At different times in our history the Central American States have looked to annexation as the only relief from chronic revolution. Whatever difference of opinion there may be with regard to the policy of annexation, there can be no difference with regard to the increased power and influence in the West Indies such intimate daily communication and such additional commercial facilities will give to the United States. If the iron rail binds the Atlantic and Pacific coasts together, so will the opening of this line of communication in the same way cement Cuba and the other West Indies to us in peace and amity, and indissoluble commercial relations.

The following is the amount and value of sugar raised in Cuba, and the sum paid for freights between Havana and the United States, on sugar imported :

During 1873 the production of sugar in Cuba was 690,000 tons, of which 441,000 tons—64 per cent.—together with 180,000 tons of molasses, went to the United States. This constituted 80 per cent. of the foreign sugar and 90 per cent. of the molasses consumed by the American people for the year. That is to say, 30 out of every 40 pounds of sugar used per capita in the United States in 1873 were supplied from the island. Nor is this dependence upon the one cheap source of supply likely to be less extreme hereafter, while the amount of sugar required must increase enormously every year. Ten years ago the amount consumed in the United States was but twenty pounds per capita—a vast increase of consumption, wholly irrespective of the increase of population.

In 1873 not less than 441,000 tons of Cuban sugar were exported to the United States ; the same was valued at $77,500,000 which was in excess of the importations from France into the United States the same year, $44,500,000. Furthermore, these Cuban imports gave an exceptional earning of $4,000,000 to American shipping. Here, assuredly, is the most conclusive evidence of the vital concern which Cuban sugar production is to the business interests of the American people.

THE COMMERCE OF THE VALLEY OF THE OHIO AS RELATED TO THE GREAT SOUTHERN RAILWAY.

The information herein, is derived, mainly from the report. of the "*Select Committee of the Senate on transportation routes to the sea board,*" and from the report of the Chief Engineer U. S. Army.

This report of the Select Committee, is the result of the most comprehensive investigation ever made in the United States, of the internal commerce of the nation.

The information embodied in the following extracts, relates only to that commerce, to and from the valley of the Ohio, seeking transit by the quickest and cheapest route to its destination, over the—this Railway. The statements and the statistics herein given are by the highest authority to which we can go.

We will say preliminary to what is hereinafter given, that this Railway has two Southern termini, viz: Turtle Harbor and Key West. Turtle Harbor being at the southeast of the Southern end of the peninsula of Florida, and Key West being the southwest key of the Florida Keys, and 116 miles south and west of Turtle Harbor. Turtle Harbor ha 27 feet of water, over the bar at low tide and Key West Harbor 32 feet.

Either harbor can be entered by day or by night at all seasons of the year, and in all weathers, by sail or steam, directly from the ocean, without the aid of a pilot or towage. Either harbor being always available for the largest merchant ships, and naval vessels, of the world. Two harbors, more available, and more perfectly adapted for the safety of ships, and the facilities of commerce, do not exist.

The distance from the Saint Mary's River to Turtle Harbor is 450 miles; from Turtle Harbor to Key West, 116 miles, *i. e.:* from the Saint Mary's River to Key West, 566 miles. These ports are both reached by this Railway and thus are connected via the Florida peninsula with the railroad system of the United States. At Jacksonville and Callahan in Florida; at Waynesville, Jesup and Millen in Georgia; this road makes connection with the whole system of roads, in the country, and is, of itself, a continuous line of road, from Millen, Georgia to Key West, Florida. At Jesup it connects with the Macon and Brunswick railroad and by it makes its through connections to Louisville, Kentucky and Cincinnati, O. It is this line from Louisville and Cincinnati via Chattanooga, Atlanta, Macon and Jesup to Turtle Harbor, and Key West, and connections, that we intend to discuss under this head.

New Orleans, as is shown by the Senate Report, is now the second port in value of commerce in the United States, and even so while it had less than 16 feet of water, at the mouth of the Mississippi river. The city of New Orleans is 510 miles from the port of Key West by water, thus giving Key West an advantage of 510 miles over New Orleans in ocean transportation, and Turtle Harbor an advantage over New Orleans of 725 miles; and in the latter case all danger to vessels from the Florida reefs, is avoided; as the carriage is made by rail on the line of the Florida keys. Thus, in point of fact, railroad transportation is carried 510 miles at Key West, and 775 at Turtle Harbor, further south than at New Orleans. From Savannah to Turtle Harbor is 446 miles, and to Key West 557 miles by ocean transportation, thus saving by the Atlantic coast in ocean transportation 441 miles to Turtle Harbor and 557 to Key West, and from the east the dangerous passage of the Florida reefs is also saved; the railroad superceding it. From the port of New it is 1029 miles to Turtle Harbor, and 1,155 to Key West.

The following facts then present themselves. Key West is 510 miles by rail nearer than New Orleans, and Turtle Harbor 557 miles by rail nearer than Savannah to all the West India islands, to Central America, to the Panama Railroad, to Yucatan, to the islands and coast of the Carribean Sea, to the northern and eastern coast of the Continent of South America, and via Panama Railroad, the entire western coast of South America, of Central America, of Mexico; and of the United States, and of all the commerce of the Pacific Ocean seeking an eastern market, via the Panama Railroad.

We shall confine ourselves mainly to one subject, or branch of the subject i. e.: the magnitude of the freights from the states west of the Alleganies, and bordering north and south on the Ohio River. The distance ⸢from Louisville to Turtle Harbor is 1,127 miles, and Cincinnati about the same; from Louisville or Cincinnati to Key West 1,244 miles. Louisville and Cincinnati are not only the geographical centers, but the commercial center of the commerce of the seven States of the Ohio valley, viz. : Pennsylvania, West Virginia, Ohio, Kentucky, Indiana, Illinois, and Missouri. The distances of the principal grain markets of the west by rail to New York are as follows : Chicago, 987 miles ; St. Louis, 1,219; Louisville, 997. From New York to Turtle Harbor is 1,029 miles; from New York to Key West 1,155 ; from Louisville or Cincinnati to Turtle Harbor 1,127 ; and Key West 1,244.

The magnitude of the grain trade in the United States is here given from the Senate report,

"The total movement of grain from the Western states, eastward in 1872, was 178,021,462 bushels ; and Southward 35,000,000 bushels."

Relative to the exports of grain from the United State southward.

" The markets of the West Indies and South America take about 15 per cent. of the entire foreign exports from the United States."

The following table gives the shipment of grain from the United States for 1873.

Wheat, wheat flour, corn, rye, oats and barley, 1873.

Countries to which Exported.	Bushels.	Per cent.
Great Britain....................	78,313,335	84.1
West Indies, Central and South America..................	8,596,968	9.3
All other countries..............	6,107,710	6.6
Total.........................	93,018,013	100.

The railway company will employ a sufficient number of its own ships to transport all freights passing over its road to and from the Panama Railroad, the West India Islands, Central America and the islands and coast of the Caribbean Sea, and the eastern ports of South America.

And in this connection, in which mixed lines, that is, rail and water will be extensively employed, we insert the following quotation, as showing the extent to which this mode of transportation is carried, and the success which has elsewhere attended it.

The organization of mixed lines, consisting of lake steamers and railroads. The mixed lines are constituted as follows :

The Northern Transportation Company connects with the Central Vermont Railway at Ogdensburg, and is managed by the officers of that road.

The Grand Trunk or Sarina line of steamers runs in connection with the Grand Trunk Railroad, receiving freight at Chicago and delivering it to the railroad at Sarina.

The Western Transportation Line of steamers connects with the New York Central Railway at Buffalo, where its freights, if not otherwise consigned, are delivered to that road.

The vessels of the Union Steamboat Company run from Chicago to Buffalo, where they connect with the Erie Railway.

The boats of the Anchor line of propellers run from Chicago to Erie and Buffalo, where they connect with the Empire Fast Freight Line and the Pennsylvania and.Erie Railways."

The opinion of the committee is that a railroad cannot be injured by competition of water transportation.

"Another result of water lines may be briefly noted here, namely, the incidental increase in the traffic by rail. Perhaps the most successful and prosperous railway in the United States is that which extends nearly 500 miles along the Erie Canal and Hudson River. The business created by the water line creates a traffic in articles which require speedy transport and which can bear rail rates. In like manner the railway passenger traffic is largely increased. While, therefore, the whole country is benefitted by the water lines, the railways themselves share in the general prosperity. Instead of there being an antagonism between water lines and railways, they are really helpful to each other."

As the roads in the northern portion of the United States are frequently retarded by the storms and snows of winter, and as the this railway traverses a country below a paralel of lattitude, where such storms can retard the working of the road, we call attention to the conclusions of the Senate Committee, on that subject.

"The General Superintendent of traffic on the Vermont Central railroad, estimates that the cost of transportation, in the winter on their road is from 70 to 75 per cent. more than in summer. He states also that in some cases the cost of clearing the track after a single snow storm is greater than the receipts for transportation for freights for a month.

The master of transportation, on the Baltimore and Ohio railroad, says: The estimated increase cost of transportation, during the winter months, above that of the three summer months, on the Baltimore and Ohio railroad, is from 5 to 20 per cent. ranging according to the character of the power employed, the direction of the traffic the relative altitude above tide water of the portion of the road carried over, and the severity of the winter."

The extent of the commerce is here shown of the nations of the South to which this railway is the shortest, most direct, safest and cheapest channel of transportation, and which it approaches by 510 miles nearer than any other railroad or any other port in the Gulf of Mexico, and 557 miles nearer than by any other railroad or port on the Atlantic coast.

The committee recommend that the United States secure modifications in the several treaties, in such manner as to insure an increase of the commerce between the United States and these several Southern nations.

"Some idea of the possible development of the trade with these countries and islands may be formed by referring to their statistics of population, our commerce with them, and their total commerce with all other foreign countries.

Population.

Mexico	9,175,000
Central America	2,665,000
South America	28,259,000
West Indies	4,000,000
Total	44,099,000

Value of our Imports from, and our Exports to Mexico, Central America, the West Indies and South America.

Countries.	Value of Exports.	Value of Imports.
Mexico	$18,566,154	$6,430,163
Central America	2,238,896	1,347,549
West Indies	103,006,026	35,059,372
South America	75,988,998	29,641,967
Total	$199,800,074	$72,479.051

It appears that the balance of trade with these countries during the year ending June 30, 1873, was against us by the sum of $127,479,051. The value of our exports having amounted to only 36 3-10 per cent. of the value of imports.

But the possibilities of commerce with these countries are indicated by comparing the value of our trade with them with the value of their total commerce with all foreign countries.

Statement showing the Value of the total Commerce, Exports and Imports of Mexico, Central America, the West Indies, and South America with the United States and with all other Countries.

	Value of Total Commerce.	Value of Commerce with the United States.
Mexico	$25,000,000	$24,696,317
Central America	11,500,000	3,586,445
West Indies	250,000,000	138,065,434
South America	450,000,000	105,630,966
Total	$736,500,000	$271,979,162

Table showing the value of the commerce of Great Britain with Mexico, Central America, the West Indies and South America during the year 1872 :

Countries.	Value of Imports into Gr't Britain.	Value of Exports from Gr't Britain.
Mexico, (in gold)..........	$2,158,409	$4,377,610
Central America............	6,335,866	2,436,067
West Indies...............	52,239.930	33,250,137
South America.......:....	128,875,189	123,710,792
Total.................	$189,609,344	$163,774,606

The total value of the commerce of these countries and colonies, and the value of their commerce, with Great Britain and the United States may be stated as follows ;

Countries.	Value in Currency.	per cent.
Commerce with Great Britain.....	397,560,308	.54
" " United States.....	272,279,162	.37
" " All other countries.	66,660,530	.9
Total commerce..............	736,500,00	100

The lesson which these statistics convey needs no further elaboration here.

With such facts before them, the committee do not hesitate to recommend that our government shall at once adopt measures to establish more advantageous relations with the countries above named, and especially such measures as will tend to increase the amount of our exports of grain and other farm products to them. The improvement of the Mississippi river and the consequent development of a large commerce at New Orleans, will tend to bring us into close relations with them ; and thereby give to us that share of their trade to which our geographical position entitles us.

The incalculable superiority which Turtle Harbor and Key West have over New Orleans, situated as it is 105 miles above the mouth of the Mississippi river, and with less than 16 feet of water on the bar, may be seen when we know that either of the former harbors can be entered from the open sea, day or night, without pilot or towage. The Senate Committee says :

" The heavy tax imposed upon the commerce by the organization known as the Tow-Boat Association, also contributes very largely to the embarassments of the Mississippi river trade. The president of the Association testified : That the charge for towing in and out is from $1.40 to $1.50 per ton, amounting on a 2,000 ton vessel to $2,800 to $3,000 a trip."

The Committee, say of the port of New Orleans, and the vast traffic it controls despite the many hindrances it is subject to.

"And yet, notwithstanding all these disadvantages and embarassments, New Orleans is in value of her imports and exports, the second commercial seaport in the United States, her commerce being surpassed only by New York. In shipping, she is the third port, her tonnage being exceded only by that of New York and Boston ; her present commercial rank attained under all these adverse circumstances indicates the bright future that awaits her."

In this connection the depth of water on the bar, from March 8, to June 15, 1873 is given.

" Depth of channel at the mouth of the Mississippi river :

Date.	Depth, Inches. Feet.	Date.	Depth, Inches. Feet.
Mch. 8, 1873..	18....00	Mch. 29, 1873..	15....00
" 10, " ..	18....00	May, 2, " ..	17....00
" 12, " ..	16.... 6	" 6, " ..	17....00
" 15, " ..	16....00	" 18, " ..	17....00
" 22, " ..	17....00	June, 15, " ..	17.... 6
" 26, " ..	16....00		

The official statistics of the depth of water in the Savannah river at and below Savannah will be appropriate here.

The following is taken from the report of the Chief Engineer, U. S. A., of October 12, 1872.

The city of Savannah is located on the Savannah river, 18 miles above the mouth.

"The present depth at mean low water on the bar at the mouth of the Savannah river, is about 18½ feet with a mean rise and fall of 7 feet.

The mean rise and fall of tide, at the city of Savannah, is 6½ feet. Vessels drawing 22 feet of water can cross the bar on the top of the flood without striking when there is a considerable sea on, and in calm weather a draft of 23½ feet, as a maximum can be safely carried over. In spring tides this may be increased to 24½ feet, but in neap tides, must be limited to 22½ feet. To enable this draft to be carried to Savannah on the flood tide would require a depth at mean low water of 17½ feet.

The present channel is only 10 feet deep at low water, in several places and for considerable distances, so that 7½ feet of dredging is necessary to enable the largest vessels that can cross the bar to make the wharves of the city. The length of channel in which dredging would have to be made, is about 11 miles, or two thirds of the entire distance from Tybee Roads to the city."

Notwithstanding these hindrances at the Harbor of Savannah, the large commerce the city enjoys is shown by the following summary from tabular statements, given in the report of Gen. Humphreys, above named. The full tabular statements are too lengthy to copy and only the footings or totals are given.

Summary.—Value of imports brought from foreign countries into the customs district of Savannah, Georgia for the year 1871, $900,355. The value of exports to foreign countries from Savannah, Georgia for 1871, $20,026,795.

The number of vessels and tonnage [engaged in the coastwise trade entered at Savannah for 1871, vessels, 465 ; tons 323,198.

The number and tonnage of vessels engaged in the coastwise trade cleared from Savannah for 1871, number of vessels, 505; tons, 327,171.

The number and tonnage of foreign vessels, entered from foreign countries into Savannah for 1871, number of vessels, 93 ; tons, 56,820.

The number and tonnage of foreign vessels cleared for foreign countries from Savannah for 1871, number of vessels 131 ; tons, 79,402.

The number and tonnage of American vessels entered into Savannah from foreign countries for 1871, number of vessels, 52 ; tons, 33,228.

The number and tonnage of American vessels cleared for foreign countries from Savannah for 1871, number of vessels, 79 ; tons, 55,505.

Showing the quantities of cotton, lumber, domestics, wool, hides, and rice, shipped from Savannah to ports within the United States for 1871 : Cotton, bales, 116,960 ; lumber, m. feet, 12,836 ; domestics, bales, 4.477 ; wool, bales, 1,502 ; hides, 68,524 ; rice, casks, 8,211."

Referring again to the bar at the mouth of the Mississippi river, the Senate Committee, in the body of its report, makes the following statement :

" The practical results of the means applied, are stated in the report of the Board of Engineers, dated January 13, 1874. The period of time, referred to in the report, was from July 1, 1872, to April 1, 1873. *Result* width of channel from 50 to 150 feet, depth of channel 13 to 20 feet."

In our comparisons of the availability of the Harbor, of Turtle Harbor and Key West with New Orleans, we take into consideration, the engineering work now being performed by Captain Eads, carried out upon the jetty system at a cost to the Government of the United States of $20,000,000, and yet, when this vast amount of money has been expended, the city of New Orleans is 105 miles from the mouth of the river, and the cost of towage will be the same tax on commerce, as it was in 1873, and previously. Larger vessels, will be enabled to enter the river after Capt. Eads shall completed his work, than before, but aside from this, all the hindrances and drawbacks to commerce, will exist, the same as before. While the two southern harbors reached by this Railway will always be open, and a single bar of a few hundred feet, is all that separates them, or either of them, from the open sea. Turtle Harbor having at low tide 27 feet, and at high tide 32 feet, over the bar, and Key West at low tide, with 32 feet, and at high tide 37 feet, and this depth of water available on every day in the year. Two finer harbors do not exist in the United States than are reached by the southern termini of this road, and in either of which all the naval and merchant vessels of the United States, could at once ride at anchor.

The magnitude of the internal commerce of the country, seeking an outlet and market, directly north and south, may be in a degree comprehended, by the committee's statement given below.

"An idea of the magnitude of this commerce, may, however, be formed, when it is considered, that the value of the commerce of the cities and towns, on the Ohio river, amounts to the enormous sum of $1,353,000,000. The national Government has provided no means of arriving at a knowledge of such important facts, as this, in regard to the internal commerce of the country."

In this paper we have given Louisville, Kentucky, and Cincinnati, Ohio, as the centres of commerce of the valley of the Ohio, and as the cities to which this railway has its nearest and most direct connection. We have given the distance between Louisville and Cincinnati and the southern termini of the road. We will now give the Senate Committee's statement of the commerce of the cities on the banks of the Ohio river, Louisville and Cincinnati being the great centres of the traffic and commerce of all the territory designated.

"The Ohio river, from Pittsburgh to its mouth, at Cairo, is 967 miles in length. Six States border upon it, viz. : Pennsylvania, West Virginia, Ohio, Kentucky, Indiana and Illinois, and the territory embraced by it is 214,000 square miles. An elaborate statement of the commerce of the cities and towns of the Ohio river was prepared in the year 1868, by Milner Roberts, U. S. Engineer, which statement is here presented, with certain modifications, in relation to the cities of Pittsburgh, Cincinnati and Louisville, which are based upon the statistics of trade of these cities during the year 1872 :

Pittsburgh, Pa.	$30,000,000
Wheeling, W. Va.	30,000,000
Pomroy, Ohio	8,000,000
Ironton, Ohio	5,000,000
Steubenville, Ohio	8,000,000
Portsmouth, Ohio	12,000,000
Maysville, Ohio.	8,000,000
Ripley, Ohio	5,000,000
Cincinnati, Ohio	518,000,000

Madison, Ind....	12,000,000
Jeffersonville, Ind.......	5,000,000
Louisville, Ky.....................	424,000,000
New Albany, Ind.........................	15,000,000
Evansville, Ind.........	12,000,000
Wabash River........................	15,000,000
Smithland, Ky...........	30,000,000
Paducah, Ky...........	40,000,000
Cairo, Ill....	20,000,000
354 other points........	156,000,000

Total.......................... ....$1,353,000,000

These statements are the best that could be obtained. It is probable, however, that the total value here stated is less than the actual value of the commerce of the towns mentioned, as the increase of the population and commerce of the Ohio River has been very rapid since 1868, when Mr. Roberts' report was made. Only an official census could enable the committee to arrive at an accurate statement in relation to the subject."

The committee, speaking of the mineral resources of the valley of the Ohio, and more particularly of coal, says :

" The bituminous coal area of the United States is given at 133,132 square miles in the geological survey, so far as published, while Great Britain, France and Belgium contain but 14,096 square miles, or but a little over one-tenth. Of this 133,132 square miles of bituminous coal deposit, the Ohio states contain 100,000.

The relation of coal to manufactures is too well understood to need comment, to show where the manufacturing population will be in the future. The value of minerals and manufactures, to the wealth of a nation, has been too clearly demonstrated in the national life of Great Britain, to require argument to show what one hundred thousand square miles of coal will be to the seven*Ohio states, if only eleven thousand have been of such incalculable value to Great Britain. What food, what transportation then, will not this national workshop need for its workers."

The committee furnish the following statistics, showing the production and amount consumed of grain in the United States, and the amount exported from them :

" Statement showing the production of cereals in the United States, quantity consumed, and quantity exported, 1865 to 1872—

Year.	Production. Bushels.	Consumed in U. S. Bushels.	Exported. Bushels.
1865	1,127,459,185	1,100,178,958	27,280,227
1866	1,342,570,666	1,309,233,590	33,337,075
1867	1,329,729,400	1,298,147,835	31,581,565
1868	1,450,758,900	1,411,070,840	39,388,060
1869	1,491,412,100	1,458,399,134	33,012,966
1870	1,629,027,600	1,571,737,079	57,290,521
1871	1,528,776,100	1,464,070,299	64,705,801
1872	1,656,198,100,"		

The following letter, giving statistics of productions of the Ohio Valley, taken in connection with the fact that this railway is the only direct line between it and the 44,000,000 people in the nations south of Turtle Harbor and Key West is significant.

" Letter addressed to the Chairman of this Committee by Geo. H. Thurston, Esq., of Pittsburg, in regard to the improvement of the Ohio River :

PITTSBURG, October 1, 1873.

SIR :

*   *   * By the census of 1870, we find that the seven Ohio Valley States had in that year 13,459,377 inhab⸗

itants, while the eighteen States having territory bordering
on the sea coast had 15,921,352 of a population. In 1830,
when the future necessity of the* improvement of the Ohio
began to be urged, the seven Ohio States had 4,156,033 inhabitants. The eighteen sea coast States had 8,288,651. In
forty years, the census of 1870 shows the growth of population in the sea coast States had been but little over 90 per
cent., while that of the Ohio States had been a little over 200
per cent. At the same ratio, at the end of another forty
years, the sea coast States will have 30,269,189 inhabitants,
and the Ohio States 40,258,131. Should the progress of the
nation be as great then in the next forty years as in the past,
and the indications are that it may be greater instead of less,
the seven Ohio States, in population and by analogy of rea-
soning in wealth, will be as powerful an empire in all respects as the whole United States now is. What, then, will
be the wants of those States for transportation? What that
of the other States of the Union? What should the Ohio
River be made in view of this?   *   * ⁻ *

But let us look a little into the increase in the wealth of
the country of the Ohio Valley during the past twenty years
only.

In 1850, the valuation of property, real and personal, of
the seven States of the Ohio was $2,089,002,652 : in 1860 it
was $5,171,501,897 ; in 1870 it is given in the census at $10,-
726, 839,301. The valuation of the whole United States was
only $30,068,518,507: In the eighteen sea coast States
the valuation in 1850 was given at $4,324,577,745 ;
in 1860 it was stated at $8,030,198,734, and in
1870, according to the census, it is $14,229,392,289. From
this it would seem the valuation of property in the seven
Ohio States has increased in the past ten years over one hun-

dred per cent., and in twenty years over five hundred per
cent., while in the sea coast States it has increased only
seventy-five per cent. in the past ten years, and about three
hundred and thirty per cent. in twenty years, including in
that period of time California, with her great mineral development. Under the same ratio of increase as in the past ten
years, the census valuation of the Ohio States will be in 1890,
or but a little over 16 years from now, over $32,000,000,000 ;
more than ten times our national debt. This is allowing our
increase to be, from 1870 to 1880, the same per cent. as from
1860 to 1870, and from 1880 to 1890, only one-half of that per
cent. At the same period, the seacoast States would, under the
same ratios, be given at a little over $30,000,000,000. It will
easily be seen from these statistics how soon the seven Ohio
States will as much exceed the eighteen sea coast States in
wealth as they will in population.

The improvement of the Ohio is not merely a question of
the transportation wants of the 13,000,000 people inhabiting
now the seven Ohio States, with property valued now at
$10,000,000,000, important as the question is under such
figures ; but it is a question, inside of sixteen years, of over
25,000,000 of sectional population, and $30,000,000,000 of
property.   *   *   *   *   *

The bituminous coal area of the United States is given at
133,132 square miles in the geological survey so far published.   *   *   One hundred thousand square miles
will be in the seven Ohio States.   *   *   *   *

How far this magnet of fuel is concentrating in
the Ohio States, the manufacturing interests of the
nation, the comparative statistics of the number of
the manufacturing establishments, and their products, in the 18 sea coast states, and the 7 Ohio states in

1850, and in 1870, indicate. In 1850, there were according to the census, in the 18 seacoast states, 65,273, manufacturing establishments, producing $639,771,163. In 1860, there were 66,959, producing $1,121,303,395. In the 7 Ohio st ates, in 1850, there were 36,277 factories, yielding $284,452,69 6, in products. In 1860, there were 49,099 factories, yielding $568,188,147. In 1870, the census gives 101,580 manufactories, in the seacoast states, yielding $2,237,236,305 products, and in the 7 Ohio states, 97,568 factories, yielding products to the value of $1,408,916,550. From these census statistics, it appears that the increase in the 18 seacoast states, has in 20 years, been 36,307 factories, and $1,597,465,138 in product. While in the 7 Ohio States, the increase, was 63,291 factories, and $1,124,483,854 in product. It is obvious, that the factories of the Ohio States, being of more recent existance, were of less magnitude than the older ones of the Eastern Coast, including the mammoth manufacturing corporations of New England, and of course of less productive capacity. It will be observed, that the rates of increase, in the Ohio States, is about 175 per cent., and only about 56 per cent. in the 18 seacoast states, or as, *three to one*, while the increase in products, is only 25 per cent. less than in the older manufacturing sections. Under the ratio of increase of the last 10 years, only, there will be, in the 7 Ohio States in 20 years from 1870, over 250,000 factories. Their productions, taking only the average indicated by the census of 1870, will be $3,600,000, or 50 per cent. more, than the whole imports and exports, of Great Britain, to and from all countries.

It is for the manufacturing wants, of this wonderful manufacturing empire, surpassing in extent, that of Great Britain, Belgium and France, the three great manufacturing fields of

Europe, as seven to one, that the improvement of the navigation of the Ohio river is of such national importance."

The following extract is applicable as showing the immense resources for population, productions of the soil, manufactures and commerce opened by this Road, as its very chief route of transportion. The committee assert in their report that in a very few years the nations south of the United States, judging from their present increase, will contain 100,-000,000 of people, and with their most fertile and productive country at one terminus of this Road, and the vast resources of the valley of the Ohio at the other, with no rival line possible, the future of the Road must be almost beyond computation successful. No where in this paper is the imagination drawn upon, but all the statements are from official data, and the future growth of the United States and nations of the south is officially estimated from official statistics of past development and growth.

The valley of the Mississippi, as mentioned below, includes the valley of the Ohio, as its most important territorial portion, in population, wealth and commerce.

"The valley of the Mississippi,which by opening of the water routes, will become connected with the valley of the Saint Lawrence, and tributary to the commerce of the Lake countries, contains 768,000,000 acres of the finest land on the face of the globe, enough to make more than 150 states as large as Massachusetts; more territory than the areas of Great Britain;France, Spain,Austria, Prussia, European Turkey and the Italian Peninsula combined. If peopled as Massachusetts is it would contain five times the present population of the United States, and as France is, would hold as many people as the whole area of Europe contains, and as Belgium and the Netherlands are, with not the same danger of famine, it would contain 400,000,000 souls, largely more than one third of the population of the world."

In the report of the Senate committee the assertion is several times repeated that 37,000,000 bushels of grain are required for the domestic consumption of the Southern States. This railway passes through the center of these States, and will carry a larger per centage of this enormous amount of grain to the consumers than any other single road.

On the 17th day of August, 1877, Hon. John Sherman, Secretary of the Treasury, said in his speech at Mansfield, Ohio:

"The entire tonnage passing any given point of the Mississippi River, is now estimated to be 3,000,000 tons per annum."

EXTRACT FROM COMMERCIAL RELATIONS, 1877.

The following extracts are taken from a "letter from the Secretary of State, transmitting an annual report upon the commercial relations of the United States with foreign nations during the year 1876; giving certain data in the matter of the commerce of the United States with certain countries specified south of the United States." These extracts show certain facts in regard to our commerce with the nations south of this country, well worthy of consideration.

The letter is dated Department of State, Washington, March 1, 1877, and signed HAMILTON FISH.

Argentine Republic.—The increase in the trade of 1875 was principally with England, France, Belgium and the South American States. Trade with the United States decreased $1,572,000 from the amount of the previous year, or about 20 per cent. A large amount of the exports to the United States consisted of dry hides, and of imports from the United States lumber was the leading item in value. In 1874, the value of the lumber imported from all sources was $2,932,160, of which $2,189,403 was from the United States, and in 1875 the value was $2,071,974, of which only $1,316,570 was from this country. Of more than $17,000,000 worth of woven goods imported in 1874, the United States does not appear to have furnished over $40,000 worth, and but little of the material imported of the value of over $11,000,000 for use in the construction of railroads, telegraphs, tramways and other public works. Of more than a million dollars' worth of boots and shoes imported, only $2,000 worth was from our shops and factories. Yet, of the principal articles of import into the Argentine Republic, such as grain and provisions, iron, steel, and hardware, and woven goods, not including the finest, the

United States might contribute an abundance, and in some instances apparently at cheaper rates than other countries.

Brazil.—The commercial returns of Brazil are such as to render it impossible to make a satisfactory statement of her commerce and navigation and the interest of the United States therein. Although neither is large, both are increasing, and must become important in many ways to us.

In 1875 the total imports from this country were stated to be of the value of $7,494,491, of which goods worth less than a half a million of dollars entered under our flag. The exports to the United States were $42,586,665, of which 18,-204,385 cleared in American vessels. In 1876 the imports at Rio Janeiro, consisting mostly of flour and refined petroleum, were valued at $4,667,946, and the exports 789,304 bags of coffee, at $17,116,527. There has been no report upon the navigation at Rio for several years. Bahia, Ceara, Maranham, Pernambuco, and Rio Grande do Sul, having less than half the navigation, furnish material for the following statement:

		Entered.		Cleared.
Flag.	*No.*	*Tons.*	*No.*	*Tons.*
British........	623	537,814	660	487,000
French.	137	130,445	128	122,804
German... ...	156	83,217	153	78,927
United States..	101	108,399	390	78,803
Total......	1,017	857,875,	1,331	767,534

Under the four flags, the United States had 9 per cent. of the ships and 11.5 per cent. of the tonnage. If the navigation of the port of Rio was included, it is probable that the percentage would not be greatly changed.

Central America.—Commercial information for the year for the five states of Central America, is very limited. In 1874, out of a total foreign commerce of over $27,000,000, the part of the United States was less than $6,000,000, and that of Great Britain a little more than six, these nations leading. Until recently British traders have, during more than fifty years, monopolized the foreign trade of the country. Recently ours with it, has slowly increased. Navigation reports for the year show 77 entries of vessels under the flag of the United States, of an aggregate tonnage of 89,778 tons, and the same number of tonnage cleared—nearly double the tonnage under the British, French and German flags. This is due to the fact that the Pacific mail steamers touch twice a month at Central American ports. A large portion of their freight is taken at Aspinwall, however, in British bottoms to our own and other ports.

The foreign commerce of countries lying south of the United States on the American continent may be nearly estimated to be at the present time $520,000,000 in value, in which the United States shares to the extent of $112,250,000, not over one-third of which is transported under our own flag. This country is a seemingly uninterested spectator of the continuous and slowly successful efforts of its near neighbors, whose destinies are involved to a greater extent than are those of other portions of the world with her own, to emerge from traditional hindrances into a development which, for the interest of all, should be in sympathy with hers, and which may properly be influenced to a large extent through the peaceful operations of commerce.

Chili.—The trade of Chili for the year 1875 through the ports of Valparaiso, there being little through other ports, amounted to $72,621,455. The imports were $38,137,500, of which Great Britain furnished more than $15,000,000, and the United States a little more than $2,000,000. The exports amounted to $34,483,955, of which Great Britain took $20,000,000, and the United States only $413,000. The declared exports to this country for 1876 are nearly a million of dollars. In 1874, with a trade of nearly $75,000,000, the imports from Great Britain were over seventeen million dollars, from France seven, from Germany over three, and from the United States over two ; and of the exports, $22,000,000 went to Great Britain, $1,000,000 to France, and half a million to the United States.

Navigation under the flag of this country, no other being reported, is as follows :

	Entered.		Cleared.	
	No.	Tons.	No.	Tons.
1875	57	35,083	54	Not stated.
1876	49	35,497	45	Not stated.

	Entered.	Cleared.
Value of cargoes, 1875	$1,993,910	$430,000
" " 1876	1,638,010	140,000

United States of Colombia.—The foreign commerce of the United States of Colombia decreased considerably in 1875, on account of the disturbed condition of affairs in that government. •

The foreign trade for two years and its distribution are shown below, as follows :

	1874.		1875.	
Countries.	Imports.	Exports.	Imports.	Exports.
Great Britain	$1,956,381	$3,343,993	$2,964,976	$3,351,821
France	1,906,870	1,674,874	2,056,325	1,541,212
United States	806,644	1,556,506	767,473	1,469,973
Germany	676,442	2,635,769	606,783	3,132,530
All others	2,872,207	478,710	547,471	488,492
Total	$8,218,544	$9,689,852	$6,942,928	$9,984,028

The decrease was 24 per cent. The chief articles of importation were cloths, food articles, salt, wines and liquors, and metal manufactures; of exportation, gold and silver, in dust, bars and specie, tobacco, guano, bark, vegetable ivory and fine woods; these making in value seven-tenths of the exports.

Navigation under all flags at all ports, excepting Colon and Panama, for 1875 was as follows:

Countries.	Entered.		Cleared.	
	No.	Tons.	No.	Tons.
British..............	234	232,189	232	266,299
French..............	84	54,859	61	50,930
German.... .:.............:..	40	41,221	46	45,554
United States.............	20	12,325	18	15,296
Spanish..................	3	9,000	3	9,000
All others............... ...	475	19,041	471	18,532
Total...............	856	368,635	831	405,611

The navigation at Colon or Aspinwall has not been reported.

That at Panama for 1875, was as follows:

Flag.	Entered and Cleared.					
	Steamers.		Sail Vessels.		Total.	
	No.	Tons.	No.	Tons.	No.	Tons.
United States..	137	274,893	6	2,436	143	277,329
British........	126	143,109	3	3,882	129	146,991
Columbia and S. America.....	40	66,650	3	1,998	83	.58,648
Total.....	303	484,652	12	8,316	355	482,968

The tonnage here represented exhibits the marine activity connected with the Isthmus transit trade on the pacific side, and nearly 58 per cent. of it is under the United States flag, and is owned in a single line of steamers. On the Eastern side of the Isthmus the sea-carrying trade is more in possession of other nations, into whose hands a large proportion of the goods are reported to pass. The imports at Panama for the same year are reported as being of the value of $13,443,-000, and the exports the same.

From the Appendix of the Letter of the Secretary of State Argentine Republic, port of Buenos Ayres.—From the table given it will be seen that the total number of arrivals and departures of steamers trading with foreign ports during the year 1875 amounted each way to 975, with a total tonnage of 510,758 tons each way, representing more than one half of the entire tonnage of the Argentine Republic.

The following table shows the flag which these steamers carried.

Nationality.	Number.	Tonnage.
German	23	50,807
Belgium	4	6,027
Brazilian	59	9,708
Spanish	2	1,721
French	161	107,835
British	295	220,673
Italian	27	23,173
Argentine	225	45,693
Norwegian	4	4,029
Uraguayan	175	41,092
United States	00	00
Total	975	510,746

These steamers during the year made twenty-four voyages to Germany, fifteen to Belgium, forty-seven to Brazil, three to Spain, four hundred and fifty-eight to Uruguay, sixty-eight to France, one to Holland, one hundred and fifty-nine to

England, forty-two to Italy, one hundred and fifty-seven to Paraguay, one to Portugal, *and not one to the United States.* The total foreign commerce, imports and exports of the Argentine Republic for the year 1875 amounted to $106,097,-027, against $99.065,889 in 1874, and $116,934,513 in 1873·

The imports for 1875 amounted to $55,756,627, being $195,-550 less than the year previous. The exports amounted to $50,331,400, being an increase of $7,226,688 over 1874.

The exchanges between the Argentine Republic and Europe during 1875 represent 72.13 per cent. of the entire commerce ; those with America amount to 21.01 per cent.; those in transitu to 6.56 per cent., and those with Asia 0.30 per cent.

The following are the trade returns with the United States during the last six years :

Trade	1870	1871	1872	1873	1874	1875
Im'pts	$2,862,338	2,067,275	3.505,944	5,167,616	3,949,584	3,069,354
Exp'ts	3,827,530	3,709,357	4,312,355	3,032,945	3,747,300	3,055,205
Total	6,689,868	5,776,634	7,518,299	8,200,561	7,696,884	6,124,059

With proper effort this trade might be extended indefinitely and be made to embrace all such lines of staple manufactures as have a market in the Argentine Republic.

When all the leading countries of Europe are competing for the trade of the Argentine Republic, it is difficult to explain why it is that the United States manifests so much apathy on the subject. The first step towards securing this object should be the establishment of steamship navigation between our American ports and Buenos Ayres.

Honduras.—The fruit trade with the United States has undoubtedly increased at the rate of 33⅓ per cent. per year for last three or four years.

Americans have established a large depot at Hipiona for importation of merchandise from the United States, and it has been made a port of entry, to facilitate their business. Having good communication with the interior, the enterprise bids fair to be the means of introducing American goods and manufactures into the interior of Honduras, heretofore chiefly supplied from British sources.

Porto Rico Port of Mayaguez.—The total value of imports during the year (1875) amounted to $0,219,535, against $3,041,920, in the preceding year, showing an increase of $177,615. In imports from the United States, I note a decrease compared with those of last year, which were estimated at $640,819 while those of the present year cannot be estimated above $553,180.

Exports during the year amounted to $3,346,602, against $3,549,962, in the preceding year, showing a decrease of $203,360, chiefly owing to the low prices ruling throughout the year for sugars; the falling off in value of exports of this article, being $139,678, while that of coffee has further increased $36,455, and represents in total $1,294,533 more than the first named product.

SHIPMENTS BETWEEN NEW YORK AND SAN FRANCISCO VIA PANAMA.

The quarterly report of the Bureau of Statistics of the Treasury Department gives the shipment of commodities between New York and San Francisco via Panama, for the six quarters commencing October 1, 1875, and ending March 31, 1877, as follows:

Shipment of domestic commodities from New York to San Francisco via Panama:

October 1 to December 31, 1875	$1,332,936
January 1 to March 31, 1876	1,300,306
April 1 to June 30, 1876	775,441
July 1 to September 30, 1876	785,514
October 1 to December 31, 1876	886,656
January 1 to March 31, 1877	896,325
Total six quarters	$5,977,178

Shipment of domestic commodities from San Francisco to New York via Panama:

October 1 to December 31, 1875	$758,608
January 1 to March 31, 1876	371,597
April 1 to June 30, 1876	333,740
July 1 to September 30, 1876	366,555
October 1 to December 31, 1876	376,898
January 1 to March 1, 1877	522,846
Total for six quarters	$2,730,244

Shipments of foreign commodities from New York to San Francisco, via Panama:

October 1 to December 31, 1875	$49,879
January 1 to March 31, 1876	58,990
April 1 to June 30, 1876	14,121

July 1 to September 30, 1876................... — --—
October 1 to December 31, 1876................. 59,258
January 1 to March 31, 1877................. 46,684

Total for six quarters. $208,932
Shipment of Foreign commodities from San Francisco to
New York via Panama:
October 1 to December 31, 1875................ ....$ 3,517
January 1 to March 31, 1876.......... 0
April 1 to June 30, 1876......................... 243
July 1 to September 30, 1876..................... 0
October 1 to December 31, 1876................:... 12,547
January 1 to March 31, 1877..................... 538

Total for six quarters..................... ....$16,845
Total shipment of commodities between New York and
San Francisco via Panama for six quarters ending March
31, 1877, (18 months), $8,933,199.

COMMERCE WITH CUBA, PERU, COLOMBIA, MEX-ICO, ARGENTINE REPUBLIC, CHILI, URUA-GUAY AND BRAZIL.

The following data are taken from the reports of the Bureau of Statistics published for 1876 and 1877. Imports into the United States and foreign exports from the same, from CUBA and PORTO RICO, during the fiscal year ending June 30, 1875.

Imports.

Cuba... ....$2,480,588
Porto Rico....................•..................... 259,757

Foreign Exports.

Cuba... 5,280,140
Porto Rico................................... 11,400

Imports into the United States from CUBA and PORTO Rico during the fiscal year ending June 30, 1875.

Cuba...$66,647,270

Porto Rico.................................... 6,670,325

Foreign exports from the United States to Cuba and Porto Rico during the fiscal year ending June 30, 1875.

Cuba...$ 6,374,351

Porto Rico................................... 108,963

Domestic exports from the United States to Cuba and Porto Rico during the fiscal year ending June 30, 1875.

Cuba..$15,586,658

Porto Rico.................................. 2,377,757

Statement of merchandise exported to Peru from the United States, Great Britian and France for the year 1874.

United States.............................. ....$2,621,906

Great Britain............................. 9,149,885

France................................'............ 6,498,610

Statement of merchandise exported to the United States of Colombia from the United States, Great Britain and France for the year 1874.

United States............................;...................$ 5,359,344

Great Britain..................... 12,960,780

France........................... 4,705,695

Statement of merchandise exported to Mexico from the United States, Great Britain and France for the year 1874.

United States......................... .....$ 6,004,370

Great Britain............. 6,614,380

France..................... 4,512,708

Statement of merchandise exported to the Argentine Republic from the United States, Great Britain and France for the year 1874.

United States.................................$2,633,963

Great Britain..,............................15,961,695

France 14,775,806

Statement of merchandise exported to Chili from the United States, Great Britain and France for the year 1874. ·

United States.........;....................$2,813,990

Great Britain.............................14,462,425

France 9,269,970

Statement of merchandise exported to Uruguay from the United States, Great Britain and France for the year 1874.

United States...............................$1,147,620

Great Britain................................6,520,780

France...................... 5,795,539

Statement of merchandise exported to Brazil from the United States, Great Britain and France for the year 1874.

United States...............................$7,705,820

Great Britain..............................40,230,750

France.....................................16,658,215

Statement showing the commerce between the United States and Chili during the year ending December 31, 1875.

Exports from the United States.................$2,021,315

Imports in the United States......... 647,515

Total exports and imports......$2,668,830

Aggregate Exports of Sugar and Molasses from the Ports of the Island of Cuba from January 1 to December 31, 1875.

DESTINATION.	SUGAR.				MOLASSES.			TOTAL.	
	Boxes.	Hhds.	Tons.	Per ct.	Hhds.	Tons.	Per ct.	Tons.	Per ct.
United States......	426,000	628,793	469,219	70·98	263,211	171,087	92·55	640,306	75·70
Great Britain......	466,792	76,840	136,139	20·59	5,453	3,544	1·92	139,683	16·52
North of Europe......	22,008	305	4,370	0·66	....	....	....	4,370	0·51
France......	61,389	6,918	15,936	2·41	...	...	...	15,936	1·88
South of Europe......	165,962	1,801	32,645	4·94	87	57	0·03	32,702	3·86
Other parts......	5,550	2,744	2,749	0·42	15,623	10,155	·5·50	12,904	1·53
Total 1875......	1,147,701	717,401	661,058	....	284,374	184,843	....	845,901	....
Total 1874......	1,105,499	660,098	617,655	....	269,586	175,230	....	792,885	....
Increase 1875......	42,202	57,303	43,403	....	14,788	9,613	....	53,016	....

Statement showing the trade between the Republic of Uruguay and other Countries during the year 1873.

Countries.	Imports.	Exports.	Total.
England	$6,782,368 70	$5,336,346 89	$12,118,715 59
France........	4,853,570 74	8,206,235 37	8,059,806 11
Brazil........	1,857,811 31	1,986,553 51	3,844,364 82
United States..	1,445,477 18	1,387,793 25	2,833,270 43
Belgium......	880,879 16	1,907,141 59	2,788,020 75
Spain........	1,170,989 68	41,692 62	1,212,682 30
Italy.........	860,275 01	305,546 44	1,165,821 45
Arg'tine Rep'c.	573,680 85	560,309 37	1,133,990 22
Cuba....	360,102 07	582,545 38	942,647 45
Germany.....	872,761 95	8,665 78	881,427 73
Holland......	220,094 72	......	220,094 72
Paraguay.....	55,775 65	22,676 86	¡78,452 51
Chili........	74,763 24	3,105 10	77,868 34
Portugal.....	45,182 18	10,620 76	55,802 94
West Ind., not specified...	......	25,287 57	25,287 57
India........	398 70	2,606 60	3,005 30
Peru........	638 00	2,262 46	2,900 46
Other ports, not speci'd.	1,020,676 90	912,372 67	1,933,049 57
Aggregate .	$21,075,446 04	$16,301,762 22	$37,377,208 26

TRADE WITH SOUTH AMERICA.

STATEMENT of IMPORTS into the United States from South America during the Fiscal Year ended June 30, 1876.

	United States of Columbia.	Venezuela.	Brazil.	Argentine Republic.	Chili and Peru.	All other South American Countries.
	VALUE.	VALUE.	VALUE.	VALUE.	VALUE.	VALUE.
TOTAL IMPORTS............	$5,497,646	5,875,715	45,453,173	3,602,736	2,196,195	1,932,539
Portion brought in American Vessels.........	3,608,314	2,649,341	14,345,885	3,290,942	861,236	1,264,454
Portion brought in foreign Vessels..........	1,889,332	3,226,374	31,107,288	311,794	1,334,959	668,085

STATEMENT of DOMESTIC EXPORTS from the United States to South America during the Fiscal Year ended June 30, 1876.

	United States of Columbia.	Venezuela.	Brazil.	Argentine Republic.	Chili and Peru.	All other countries in S. America.
	VALUE.	VALUE.	VALUE.	VALUE.	VALUE.	VALUE.
GRAND TOTAL............	3,946,442	3,424,278	7,253,218	1,519,190	3,334,674	1,126,123
Shipped in American vessels............	3,324,013	2,431,992	4,442,006	1,076,991	2,356,228	457,955
Shipped in foreign vessels............	622,399	992,286	2,811,212	442,199	978,446	668,168

STATEMENT of FOREIGN EXPORTS from the United States to South America during the Fiscal Year ending June 30, 1876.

COMMODITIES.	U.S. of Columbia [New Granada and Panama.]	Venezuela.	Brazil.	Argentine Republic.	Chili and Peru.	All other countries in S. America.
	VALUE.	VALUE.	VALUE.	VALUE.	VALUE.	VALUE.
TOTAL FOREIGN EXPORTS............	164,804	57,209	94,162	65,862	72,934	11,470
Portion shipped in American vessels...........	148,893	46,113	53,478	60,049	32,945	6,516
Portion shipped in foreign vessels...........	15,911	11,186	40,684	5,813	39,989	4,954
TOTAL COMMERCE............	9,608,892	9,357,292	52,800,553	6,187,789	5,603,803	3,070,132

Total Commerce with South America....... $85,628,420.
Portion shipped in American vessels....... 40,462,337.
Portion shipped in foreign vessels .... 45,166,183.

An editorial in the New York *Herald* of July 18, 1877, makes the following statement :

We have more machinery of all kinds than we ever had before ; we have more skilled mechanics and artisans ; the ingenuity of our people has perfected labor-saving processes in every department of production. And the result of all this is that we are poor because we are too rich ; we are suffering because our ingenuity, skill and abundant machinery enable us easily to make far more than we can use ourselves. Hence our home markets are glutted and our factories stand idle half the time. One of the broadest and most statesmanlike ideas which has ever been put forth by American public men concerns this very matter of more intimate, the most intimate, commercial relations between the United States and the nations of North, Central and South America. We are now one of the greatest manufacturing nations of the world. We use more and better labor saving machinery than any European people. None of the other nations on these two continents have yet engaged largely in manufactures. They are not, like the people of Europe, our competitors. They produce mainly the raw materials of industry and exchange these for manufactured products. They must continue for many years to do so, and they affoid an almost illimitable market for our manufactures, if only we are wise and far-sighted enough to use our advantages.

A few figures will show how great are the opportunities which we have so long neglected for building up a market for our surplus manufactures in this hemisphere. Of the total imports of Mexico, amounting to over $30,000,000, we send her only $5,000,000. Canada imports about $130,000,000 per annum, but takes only $34,000,000 from us, her nearest neighbor. Brazil imports about $85,000,000, but takes a beggarly $7,000,000 of our products, though we buy to the amount of $35,000,000 from her. Chili imports about $40,000,000, but takes only $2,000,000 of our manufactures. The Argentine Confederation imports to the value of $54,000,000 a year, but buys of us only $1,500,000. The account, is as one-sided in almost all the South and Central America countries. They buy elsewhere, mainly because they sell their raw materials elsewhere. From Chili. for instance, we bought in 1876 only to the value of $586,000 worth, while her total exports amounted to over $35,000,000. The total exports of the Argentine Confederation amount to over $50,000,000, of which we buy about $4,000,000. It is easy to see that there is something wrong in all this. We neither buy nor sell as our skill, the excellence and variety of our products and the enterprise of our people would lead us to expect; and when we look over the figures representing the total imports of these countries, who are our neighbors and our natural allies, no one can help seeing what an immense opening there is right here at our doors for the sale of our surplus products.

We can do without Europe ; we need not seek to sell a yard of cloth or a pound of any manufactured articles in Europe, if only we can command, as we ought, the great and growing commerce of North and South America. Why should we continue to buy nearly $100,000,000 worth of Cuban products and sell to the island, under a ridiculous, oppressive and antiquated commercial treaty, less than $14,000,000 worth of our products? It is unreasonable. Why should we continue to sell to sell to Brazil only $7,000,000 of her $83,000,000 of imports? We ought to be able to quadruple our sales to her with ease. We must sell our surplus before good times can be brought back. Every merchant and manufacturer knows that even so small a surplus as ten per cent beyond the power of the country to consume is enough to crush every industry.

The following appeared in the financial items of the New York *Tribune*, August 1, 1877:

The importations of sugar this Summer are immense, and the exportations small. In eleven months the importations have been 1,329,944,035 lbs., against 1,233,060,717 lbs., in the corresponding period last year, and they have been made at 5 cents a pound, as against 4 cents last year. The export been about 36,000,000 lbs. Last year in the same period it was 56,000,000 lbs.

OUR SOUTH AMERICAN COMMERCE.

Extract from New York *Herald*, August 18, 1877.

This country ought to have the largest share of the commerce of American States south of us from the Rio Grande to the Rio de la Plata. We produce in great abundance the commodities which those communities need, and by proximity of geographical situation we ought to command their markets for such manufactures as we can supply as cheaply as other nations. In all ordinary cotton goods, for example, we are in a position to compete with any nation in the world, so far as the trade depends on the quality and prices of the fabrics. And yet England has almost a monopoly of those extensive and profitable markets. The only reason why we cannot successfully compete with her is found in our lack of facilities for intercourse with the South American ports. It is not a more improved state of our manufactures that we need in order to command those large and profitable markets, but a revival and extension of our lost navigation. A difference of a fraction of a cent on a yard would enable us to capture the South American trade ; but although we can place cotton goods on a Boston wharf cheaper than England can place them on a wharf in Liverpool, she can nevertheless undersell us at Rio or any other South American port. Her regular lines of steamships enable her to supply goods as they are wanted, whereas our irregular and desultory communication by sailing vessels makes it impossible for us to pursue an advantageous trade. The cost of transportation and the uncertainty of proportioning his shipments to the demand expose the American merchant to losses to which the English merchant is not liable, and more than overbalance the superior quality and cheapness of the American goods. Our manufacturers will not have fair play until our shipping interest is revived, and it is among the clearest duties of Congress to relieve the general distress of our industries by such legislation as will rehabilitate our navigation and give us control of the extensive markets which by local position are naturally ours.

THE NORTHWESTERN WHEAT CROP.

From the New York Herald, August 24, 1877.

The Northwestern wheat crop has been a bountiful one. From statistics, it is estimated that there can scarcely be any important difference from the following figures :—

	1875.	1876.	1877.
	Bushels.	*Bushels.*	*Bushels.*
Minnesota	27,000,000	16,000,000	35,000,000
Iowa	29,000,000	18,000,000	37,000,000
Wisconsin	25,000,000	15,000,000	27,000,000
Kansas	12,000,000	12,000,000	20,000,000
Totals	93,000,000	61,000,000	117,000,000

These figures, showing that the four States above mentioned will have say 56,000,000 bushels more wheat to sell than they had last year, may be relied upon as being as near correct as the very best information can make them.

The aggregate wheat crops of Michigan, Indiana, Ohio, Kentucky and Tennessee will exceed the aggregate of last year by probably 35000,000 to 40,000,000 bushels.

The corn is late, Illinois will yield nearly 300,000,000 bushels, and Iowa not fall much, if any, short of 175,000,000 of bushels.

Table showing the Imports and Exports of the principal South American and Central American countries and the West India Islands.

IMPORTS AND EXPORTS OF PRINCIPAL CENTRAL AND SOUTH AMERICAN STATES.

Countries.	Period.	Imports.	Exports.
Argentine Republic..............	1873	$71,065,000	$45,859,000
"	1875	55,176,000	50,331,000
Bolivia (estimated)..............	1873	2,929,000	4,505,000
"	1875	5,600,000	4,870,000
Brazil...............	1872-73	77,327,000	95,261,000
"	1873-74	83,244,000	103,385,000
Chili........:...............	1873	33,945,000	34,561,000
"	1875	38,138,000	35,928,000
Costa Rica (San Salvador)........	1873	4,500,000	6,620,000
"	1875	2,850,000	4,560,000
Cuba, Port Mantanzas...........	1874	not given	17,339,000
Cardenas	1874	"	18,546,000
Sagua La Grande............	1874	"	9,852,000
Ecuador......................	1870	4,225,000	4,388,000
"	1874	....	3,914,000
Guatamala............ ..:......	1868	1,931,000	2,607,000
"	1874	3,054,000	3,189,000
"	1875	2,586,000	3,215,000
Hayti......................	1872	6,860,000	7,505,000
Honduras	1875	833,000	1,004,000
" (Estimates)............	1873	1,000,000	1,140,000
" (Estimates)............	1874	....	1,305,000

Mexico.	1872	19,993,000	18,630,000
"	1873	20,062,000	31,691,000
Nicaragua	1873	1,153,000	1,585,000
Paraguay.	1873	1,148,000	1,100,000
"	1875	566,000	608,000
Peru (Callao).	1875	17,000,000	2,415,000
Porto Rico	1872	not given.	13,928,000
"	1873	"	13,733,000
"	1874	"	11,761,000
San Salvador	1873	2,103,000	3,377,000
United States of Colombia	1872-3	12,516,000	10,961,000
Uruguay	1872	19,467,000	15,499,000
"	1874	16,600,000	16,000,000
Venezuela	1870	14,711,000	20,900,000
"	1875	12,000,000	17,000,000

Bureau of Statistics, August 7, 1877.

EDWARD YOUNG,
Chief of Bureau.

Table showing the value of Imports into the United States from, and of Domestic and Foreign Exports from the United States to the countries hereinafter named during the fiscal year ended June 30, 1876.

	Imports.	Domestic Exports.	Foreign Exports,
Central American States	$1,819,120	$938,102	$40,660
Danish West Indies	393,612	805,309	13,498
French W. I. and French Guiana	1,857,668	1,486,925	38,926
British W. I. and Brit. Honduras	3,479,291	8,197,042	223,693
British Guiana	1,172,119	1,750,452	41,838
Hayti	3,076,199	4,732,724	105,998
Dutch W. I. and Dutch Guiana	679,172	873,546	15,450
San Domingo	405,363	679,859	40,554
Cuba	58,817,689	13,746,058	2,303,874
Porto Rico	4,305,824	2,099,076	65,794
Totals	75,924,056	35,325,093	2,800,294
Total Exports	38,215,387		

Total Exports and Imports... 114,139,443

EDWARD YOUNG, Chief of Bureau.
BUREAU OF STATISTICS, August 2, 1877.   12

INTERNAL COMMERCE OF UNITED STATES.

The following several extracts, bearing directly or indirectly upon the location and objects of this road, and the prospective commerce over it, are taken from the *First Annual Report on the Internal Commerce of the United States*, by Joseph Nimmo, Jr., Chief of the Division of Internal Commerce of the Bureau of Statistics of the Treasury Department.

As the Mississippi River will be the great competitor with this road in transportation of freights from the northwest, we insert the following extract from the report as showing that water transportation is not necessarily injurious to transportation by rail. The relative importance of the railroads and the Erie Canal may be inferred from the grain receipts at Portland, Boston, New York, Philadelphia and Baltimore during the year 1876.

Received at—

		Bushels.
New York, { By canal and Hudson River		$32,853,829
{ By rail		59,047,953
Portland		3,999,181
Boston		22,753,698
Philadelphia		35,546,845
Baltimore		37,564,536
Total by rail		158,912,213

N. B.—There appears to have been about four million bushels received at New York "coastwise," which does not appear in the above table.

Almost 95 per cent. of the total receipts of grain at Boston, Philadelphia, and Baltimore, were from the Western States, a traffic in which the rail lines compete with each other and with the water-line.

The total receipts by rail and by water (including coastwise receipts) at the five ports appear to have been:

	Bushels.
By water	32,853,829
By rail	157,912,213
Total	191,766,052

It appears that 17 per cent. of the total receipts was by the Erie Canal and Hudson River and 83 per cent. by rail. It is to be observed, however, that 13,672,732 bushels of grain received "by lake" at Buffalo were thence shipped by rail. This shows that about 24 per cent. of the shipments from the West were by lake and about 76 per cent. by rail.

Tons of freight received at Saint Louis from the South and of freight shipped from that city to the South, by river and by rail, from 1871 to 1875, inclusive.

Year.	Received		Shipped		Total receipts and shipment	
	By river.	By rail.	By river.	By rail.	By river.	By rail.
1871	428,935	782,539	636,151	175,634	1,065,086	958,173
1872	419,070	1,083,600	706,381	262,246	1,125,451	1,345,846
1873	355,535	1,107,228	681,885	282,593	1,037,420	1,389,821
1874	264,105	1,020,414	577,395	301,092	841,500	1,321,506
1875	281,270	1,237,205	499,300	375,716	780,570	1,612,921

Adding receipts to shipments, it appears that the traffic to and from the South by river fell from 1,055,086 tons in 1871 to 780,570 tons in 1875, and that the traffic by rail increased from 958,173 tons in 1871 to 1,612,921 tons in 1875.

The passenger travel between Saint Louis and the South has been nearly all diverted from the river to the rail. The great bulk of first-class travel now goes by rail, it being more expeditious and more certain.

Shipments from New Orleans to Saint Louis by rail consist of tropical fruits, sugar, molasses, coffee, rice, and fancy groceries (imported). These same artices are also brought by water, and there is no class of goods except perishable, like tropical fruits, that can be said to come exclusively by rail.

Shipments from Saint Louis to New Orleans by rail are inconsiderable, and consist chiefly of live stock and meats requiring quick transit.

The Missouri, Kansas and Texas and the Iron Mountain Railroads have given Saint Louis an opportunity of forcing her trade upon Texas, though she is much farther off than New Orleans. She is not only putting groceries, dry goods, drugs, shoes, hats, and millinery goods, all brought from the East by rail, into Texas, but she is drawing away the grain and cotton. These articles are, for want of railroads to New Orleans, taken to Saint Louis, nearly double the distance it is to New Orleans, not because Saint Louis is a good market for them, for she is not, especially for cotton, but simply because Saint Louis has had the enterprise to build railroads and push a trade into Texas.

Statement showing the number of bushels of wheat (including wheat flour) exported from the United States from 1830 to 1876, to the countries named.

Year.	West Indies and Cent'l American States.	Brazil.
1830	754,880	885,312
1840	2,019,840	890,991
1850	1,549,866	1,316,088
1860	2,209,640	2,259,558
1861	2,142,197	1,640,754
1862	2,425,628	1,679,859
1863	2,828,429	1,839,690

1864	3,191,936	1,835,883
1865	3,107,501	1,650,780
1866	2,174,472	1,332,648
1867	1,588,872	751,285
1868	2,408,703	1,114,402
1869	2,931,741	1,738,814
1870	3,435,344	1,692,976
1871	3,754,029	2,050,528
1872	3,773,858	1,719,972
1873	1,441,938	1,840,716
1874	1,899,891	2,396,205
1875	1,725,293	2,799,255
1876	2,490,824	2,680,900

Statement showing the number of bushels of corn (including corn meal) exported from the United States from 1850 to 1876, to the countries named.

Year.	West Indies and Central America.	Year.	West Indies and Central America.
1850	1,656,508	1868	874,287
1860	795,557	1869	915,460
1861	878,699	1870	968,611
1862	1,100,205	1871	1,110,493
1863	955,937	1872	834,094
1864	946,957	1873	872,977
1865	886,128	1874	941,734
1866	1,034,877	1875	671,836
1867	827,046	1876	504,836

The following table indicates the total tonnage entered at
New Orleans, from 1853 to 1876, inclusive :

Year.	New Orleans. Tons.	Year.	New Orleans. Tons.
1853	511,878	1865	50,970
1854	492,434	1866	228,339
1855	435,863	1867	253,729
1856	663,067	1868	326,216
1857	612,286	1869	381,882
1858	583,776	1870	458,447
1859	659,083	1871	566,797
1860	632,298	1872	501,965
1861	68,993	1873	222,791
1862		1874	630,985
1863		1875	434,006
1864	50,588	1876	

RAILROADS SOUTH OF THE UNITED STATES.

*Statement showing the mileage of railroads in each country nam-
ed at the close of the year 1865.*

Countries and States.   Miles of Railroad
                                                        in operation.

CENTRAL AMERICA AND WEST INDIES.

Honduras	66
Costa Rica	29
Panama	49
Cuba	427
Jamaica	34
Barbadoes	6
Total Central America, &c.	611

SOUTH AMERICA.

Colombia	43
Venezuela	39
Guiana (British)	68
Brazil	837
Paraguay	47
Uruguay	197
Argentine Republic	994
Peru	972
Chili	629
Total South America	3,826
United States of Mexico	327
Total Railroads South of the United States.	4,764

UNITED STATES APPROPRIATIONS FOR PUBLIC WORKS.

Besides the aid extended by the National Government for the promotion of commerce and the development of unsettled territory, in the form of land grants and the extension of its credit in behalf of the construction of Pacific railroads, Congress has also, from time to time, since the organization of the Government, contributed largely towards the improvement of rivers and harbors, the safety of navigation, and the construction of wagon roads and canals. The value of all these aids, and the proportion which they bear to the amount of private capital expended in the construction of railroads, are matters of public interest. It appears that from the time of the adoption of the Federal Constitution until the close of the fiscal year ending June 30, 1873, the Government had appropriated in aid of public improvement the following sums :

For improvement of rivers and harbors....... $ 32,680,340

For light-houses, beacons, fog signals, marine hospitals, and other aids to navigation and commerce on navigable waters............... 16,937,115

For construction of railroads, canals and wagon roads, including bonds issued to Pacific railroads................................... 104,705,163

Estimated value of public lands granted in aid of the construction of railroads............ 52,575,150

Total aid extended to close of fiscal year ending June 30, 1873........................ $206,897,768

The total expenditures of the Government in aid of the construction of railroads, canals and wagon roads, and for the improvement of rivers and harbors and securing the safety of navigation, were, however, but five per cent. of the amount of the private capital expended in this country for the construction of railroads.

The total amount contributed by the Government in aid of railroads alone, in comparison with the total cost of the railroads of the United States, as estimated by H. V. Poor, Esq., of New York, was as follows :

Total amount of the contributions of the Government............................$ 144,213,078

Estimated cost of the railroads in the United States............................... 4,658,208,630

It appears, therefore, that the National Government had at the end of the year 1876 contributed only three per cent.

of the entire cost of the vast railroad system of the United States, all the rest being the contribution of private enterprise.

Assuming, however, that the Government had been reimbursed for the lands granted to railroad companies by the increased value of alternate sections retained, it appears that the net contribution of the Government to the entire railroad system of the country was less than two per cent. of its cost.

ADVANTAGES TO BE REALIZED FROM THE GREAT SOUTHERN RAILWAY.

This railroad connects the United States with the Islands of the West Indies, with the nations of Central America and with the nations of South America. It will practically connect the system of railroads in North America with the systems of railroads in the three divisions of the southern part of this hemisphere. It will produce a greater interchange of the productions and wealth of the tropics and semi tropics, with the United States, and it will bring within the range of the commerce of the United States, the products of their manufactories, forests, ranches, plantations, orchards, vineyards gardens, rivers, coasts, and mines. It will give an outlet to the products of our manufactories, soil and mines, still more varied and yet wholly different, from those of the tropics. It will develope a commerce, which is as broad as the commerce of the continent itself. It will bind together with a bond of friendship and mutual interests, the two halves of the continent and with them the islands of the Carribean sea. It will elevate into a higher civilization and a fuller and warmer friendship, the people of the nations of the south with our own. It will divert from Europe to this country the commerce of these nations which Europe now control.   It will afford a shorter and more rapid line of travel between this country and each and all of the countries south of it.   It will give to the United States not only one new line of commerce, but will open. scores of new lines in the undeveloped nations which it will reach by its ocean lines, and by them it will bring to our shores the untold millions of wealth which now flows to Europe.   It will permanently cheapen freights between the United States, the West Indies, Central America and South America.   It will insure the more prompt transmission of all commodities, and in even increasing quantities, to each and every part of this country.   It will give to our own people the control of the gold and silver m ines of Central and South America.   It will develop a unity of feeling between the Unites States and a score of other nations; and will so interweave the national interests, that whenever it may be the pleasure of this country to invite any one of them into the community of States, they will accept the invitation with thankfulness and each will finally add a star to our flag.

It will pass through and develope a country within our own limits, upon which Nature has lavished her choicest bounties of soil and climate.   Where the choicest forests of the country now stand, and where Nature has prepared a field upon which the sugar and fruits to supply the world may be grown when the hand of man may plant the seed.

It will develope and perfect our postal system to, and in those countries where it is now most weak and most neglected.   It will enable the Navy and War Departments to so strengthen and protect the passage of the Gulf in time of war, that no nation on earth can force the passage of the straits of Florida, or occupy the Gulf of Mexico, or occupy the mouth of the Mississippi river with a hostile fleet or army. It is the key to the military and naval occupation of the Gulf of Mexico and the Caribbean Sea. It is taken, all in all, the greatest national work now projected in the United States, and offers greater advantages to the people than any other.

SUMMARY.

The Great Southern Railway must prove one of the most valuable and profitable railway lines in the United States—
Because :

It is a direct, immediate, and the only possible railway line, stretching five hundred miles south of any other railroad between the temperate zone and the tropics of America, between 50,000,000 of people in the United States and Canada, and 44,000,000 in the West Indies, Central and South America.

Twenty per cent. of the foreign commerce of the United States is with the countries which this road and its steamship connections reach.

Eleven per cent. of the commerce of the United States is with the West Indies, which this road almost touches.

The chartered rights of the company cover the steamship lines necessary to bring this commerce over this route.

All the Central, Western and Northwestern States are nearer Havana by this line than they are to New York; hence, all traffic between these States and the tropics, even the heaviest freights will pass over this line, and ocean transportation does not come into competition.

All United States Mails for the West Indies and Central and 'South America will pass over this line, at a saving over present routes from New York of from 4 to 6 days.

All passengers to and from the countries above named will pass over this line, avoiding a sea voyage of over 1,100 miles.

All Express and Fast Freights, to and from all the United States and all the countries named, will pass this way on account of the 'saving of time and distance.

The Military Stores and Supplies for the United States forts on the Gulf of Mexico, and stores and supplies for the

Gulf, West Indies, and the South Atlantic squadrons, will reach their destination by this line.

It is the only line by which Tropical Fruits can be brought quick and fresh to northern markets.

It brings the products of Market Gardening in Florida within the available reach of New York and the north throughout the winter.

It opens the whole of Florida and Cuba to the quick and comfortable access of winter tourists and invalids.

It passes through and opens a richer and longer reach of yellow pine and live oak timber than any railroad in the United States.

It will do more business in the transportation of Sea Island Cotton than all the railroads in the United States and a large business in the northern part in Short Staple Cotton.

It reaches and opens the largest and best stocked cattle range in the United States, except in Texas, and will transport more cattle, both to the north and to Cuba, than any other road,

All the travel and traffic between all the United States and the entire peninsula of Florida will pass over this line, it being little more than half the distance, as compared with the present route by rail.

It crosses four navigable rivers and touches two others, making more than 2,000 miles of river navigation tributary to it.

Eight other completed railroads connect with it, and are so located as necessarily to give their traffic to it.

The transportation of naval stores will be greater than on any other railroad in the United States.

It has no competing railroad or river, and the geography of the country is such that it never can have.

INDEX.

A.

C.

D.

E.

F.

G.

I.

L.

M.

N.

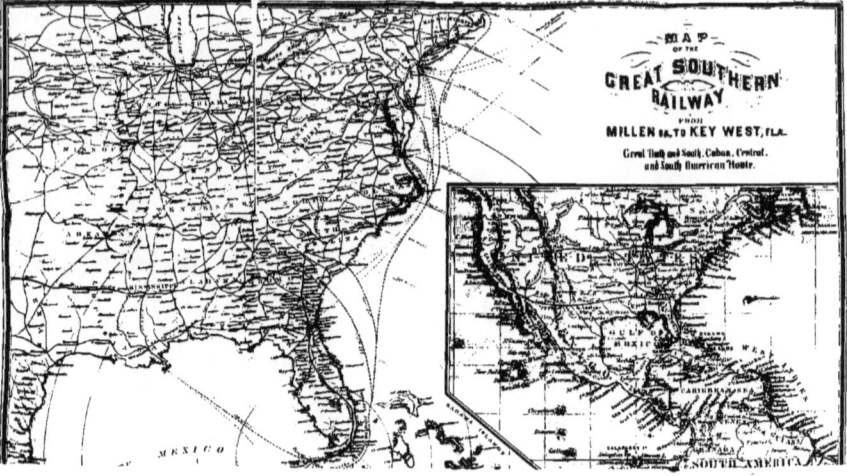

MAP
OF THE
GREAT SOUTHERN
RAILWAY
FROM
MILLEN GA, TO KEY WEST, FLA.
Great North and South, Cuban, Central,
and South American Route.

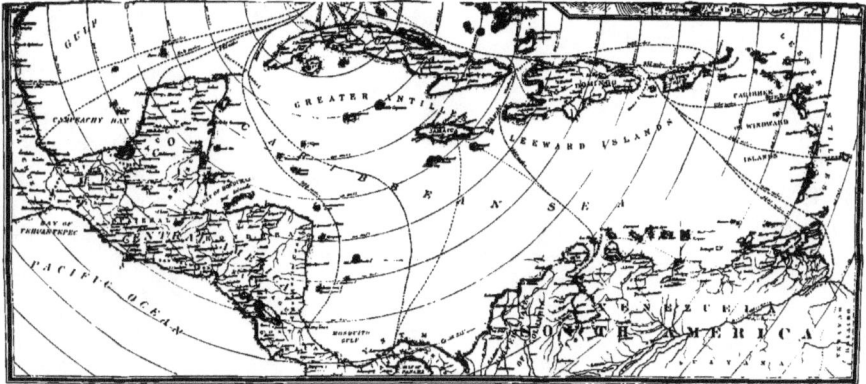

www.ingramcontent.com/pod-product-compliance
Lightning Source LLC
Chambersburg PA
CBHW030836270326
41928CB00007B/1074